Ultimate MOTORCYCLES

The Most Exotic & Exclusive Bikes on Earth

By Mark Holmes

Published by

Kandour Ltd

Monticello House

45 Russell Square

London

WC1B 4JP

UNITED KINGDOM

This edition printed in 2007

for Bookmart Ltd

Registered Number 2372865

Trading as Bookmart Ltd

Blaby Road

Wigston

Leicester LE18 4SE

First published 2007

10 9 8 7 6 5 4 3 2 1

Author: Mark Holmes
Design and Layout: Susan Holmes
Production: Karen Lomax

Special thanks to Jacs and Jimmy at Action Library (0870 062 4849)
for their help with picture research

Printed and bound in China

ISBN 13: 978-1-905741-18-2

Ultimate
MOTORCYCLES

The Most Exotic & Exclusive Bikes on Earth

By Mark Holmes

CONTENTS

INTRODUCTION

*T*he motorcycle is today's ultimate form of terrestrial transport. Try threading through the heart of any modern metropolis using any other vehicle that doesn't come fitted with flashing lights and a siren, and this will quickly become apparent. While supercars and monster SUV drivers grind their teeth in gridlock, the motorcycle can slice through the chaos of the city like a scalpel through flesh.

Short of a flying machine, the powered two-wheeler is the quickest and most efficient means of travelling from one location to another. Traffic hold-ups can be simply circumvented, train and bus timetables ignored. You don't have to stop at any place you don't need to. As long as there's gas in the tank you can go where you want.

Of course, there's much more to the motorcycle than just providing a practical conveyance. It symbolises the concept of freedom of movement and the ability to travel whenever the mood takes you. Motorcycles proved their worth as a liberating force for large sections of the

> " A skittish motorbike with a touch
> of blood in it is better than all the
> riding animals on earth "
>
> **TE Lawrence**

populations of many countries, long before the average Joe could afford four wheels to truck the family around—and they continue to provide a lifeline in many parts of the world.

But the greatest thing about motorcycles is the riding experience itself. To ride a bike is to feel the sensation of speed in its rawest form. Out there in the airstream, with the wind rushing past, the feeling is vital and visceral. The physical forces acting on the body are undiluted, the unmitigated thrill of motive power is focused and pure.

The bikes selected to appear in this book express all of these aspects of the motorcycle. Each one stands out, in its own individual way, as an ultimate two-wheeler. Whether it's a case of exotic construction, advanced engineering, acceleration, top speed, dynamic ability, sporting prowess, emotional attraction or sheer beauty, these machines are all much more than just the sum of their parts. They represent a force that breaks out of the normal confines of everyday life and can transport the spirit, as well as the body, to a better place.

EXOTIC MOTORCYCLES

Bimota DB5

Bimota SB6

Vyrus 4v

MV Agusta F4 1000

Moto Guzzi MGS-01

Hesketh V1000

Motoczysz C1

KTM RC8

Confederate Hellcat

Confederate Wraith

Honda RC30

Honda RC45

Yamaha R7

Lazareth Dokujya

Lazareth 1000 GTS

Ducati Desmosedici RR

MV AGUSTA F4

EXOTIC *Motorcycles*

Exclusive, expensive and made from high-tech materials, these bikes are some of the most desirable and outrageous on the planet. Often with radical styling and offering stupendous performance, these machines created by master craftsmen are guaranteed to stimulate the desire of bike fans all over the planet. They are the world's ultimate exotic motorcycles...

Forget the commonplace and put the run-of-the-mill far from your mind. This book of ultimate motorcycles is kicking off with some of the most desirable machines ever created—the two-wheeled world's equivalent of Ferraris, Maseratis and Lamborghinis.

In fact, that comparison is very apt, because Italy, the country that is home to the three supercar marques above, has also proved a fertile breeding ground for exotic two-wheeled vehicles.

What we're looking at in this section is a very special type of motorcycle. These are bikes made from high-tech materials, featuring the most advanced components available and often using radical construction methods. They are invariably produced in limited numbers at premium prices, guaranteeing the kind of exclusivity desired by the rich, the famous and customers who want the best, the most technologically advanced or simply the most flamboyant machines out there.

One Italian company which stands out as a creator of such high-end motorcycles is Bimota. Born in the early 1970s, the company set about taking the ever more powerful engines the Japanese were producing and slotting them into its own purpose-designed chassis. The results soon ➔

BIMOTA DB5

Introduced
2004
Engine
Air-cooled
90° V-twin
four-stroke
Capacity
992cc
Power
92bhp
Top speed
145mph

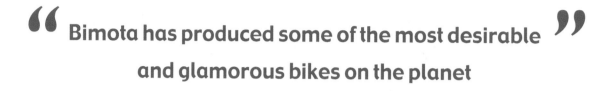

" **Bimota has produced some of the most desirable and glamorous bikes on the planet** "

→ became famous for their fine handling, especially compared to the Japanese bikes, such as Honda's 750 Four, whose engines were used to power this new breed of exotic Italian roadster.

The driving force behind the company was Massimo Tamburini, a true master of motorcycle engineering and design and a man whose name, along with the beautiful machines he has created, will crop up again later in this book.

From the '70s through the '90s, Bimota created a series of highly individual sports-focused motorcycles to the same formula as its original HB1 of 1975: take the engine from a mass-produced Japanese or Italian bike, construct a bespoke frame for it in order to maximise the machine's handling capabilities, add high-specification lightweight components and clothe the whole thing with exotically stylish bodywork.

When it was on top form, Bimota produced some of the most desirable and glamorous sports bikes on the planet, combining high technology with high performance and high prices which ensured exclusivity. One such machine was the SB6 of 1994.

BIMOTA SB6

Powered by the 156bhp four-cylinder engine from Suzuki's GSX-R1100, slightly modified with Bimota's own camshafts and exhaust system, the SB6 was capable of a top speed of 170mph. The whole bike weighed 190kg dry—decidedly featherweight for such a high-output machine of its day—helped by a state-of-the-art aluminium box-section frame.

Other components were all top-quality fare: the single horizontally-mounted rear shock absorber came from quality Swedish manufacturer Ohlins, being fully adjustable to suit the rider's requirements. Up front, the Paioli forks were impressively huge for the day, while brakes from top Italian firm Brembo provided serious decelerative force. The twin exhausts exit under the seat, with the bike's single-minded sporting nature emphasised by the fact that it has no pillion seat.   →

BIMOTA SB6

SPECIFICATIONS

Introduced
1994
Engine
In-line
four-cylinder
four-stroke
Capacity
1074cc
Power
156bhp
Top speed
175mph

The SB6 was one of Bimota's biggest successes, with the style to match its impressive performance and handling

With radical hub-centre steering and powered by the engine from Ducati's flagship 999R superbike, the Vyrus 4v is a mix of high-tech and high performance

→ When first introduced, the SB6 had unrivalled power and light weight and it became Bimota's biggest success. Over 1300 were sold – not a lot by the standards of the big Japanese factories, but a huge amount for the little company from Rimini.

BIMOTA DB5

Having gone out of business in 2000 due to the disastrous Vdue two-stroke project, Bimota was reborn with new management in 2003. Its first new product was the DB5 Mille (see previous page), first shown in 2004, and an attempt to revive the company's fortunes and status.

The recipe remains the same as for the classic Bimotas of old, in that an engine is taken from another manufacturer and fitted into a motorcycle with great flair and handling abilities. The DB5 uses Ducati's 1000DS engine, a 992cc air-cooled unit used in the company's Multistrada model. Although not hugely powerful, producing 92bhp, it is compact, torquey and road-friendly.

The frame and styling of the DB5 are more impressive than its outright performance. The frame consists of a lightweight 'trellis' of steel tubes, with connecting side plates made from aircraft-grade aluminium. Uniquely, the rear swingarm is also constructed in the same way to give great lightness and strength. The V-twin engine, with its cylinders in line with the frame, also allows the motorcycle to be very slender widthways.

PHOTOGRAPHY: CHIKO DE LUIGI

So although the DB5's top speed of 145mph is well beaten by the SB6, its handling prowess is as cutting-edge as its predecessor's was in its day. At £17,500 in the UK ($32,700) it is also one of the most 'affordable' Bimotas ever!

VYRUS 4v

One look at the photographs on these pages will tell you that this is one of the most futuristic motorcycles on the planet. In fact, it looks like a machine from another planet entirely. The Vyrus 4v takes conventional motorcycle design and turns it on its head, although it's actually based on a previous Bimota model, the limited edition Tesi 2D.

Vyrus is the company which built the Tesi for Bimota, and it now sells the 4v—essentially a development of the Tesi concept—under its own brand name. Like the Tesi, the 4v dispenses with conventional telescopic forks at the front in favour of a swingarm with suspension provided by a single pneumatic shock absorber (negating the need for a heavy spring) and a progressive linkage. The hub-centre steering system is equally radical.

While conventional forks have to work hard to perform both steering and suspension duties, the 4v's front end divides the tasks with the aim of improving the performance of both aspects. For instance, under heavy braking forks can become completely compressed, at which point they cannot deal with bumps. While braking hard into a →

VYRUS 4v

Introduced
2006
Engine
Liquid-cooled
90° V-twin
four-stroke
Capacity
999cc
Power
150bhp
Top speed
N/A

MV Agusta
F4 1000

More kinetic art than motorcycle, this Italian beauty is one of the most desirable machines in the world

SPECIFICATIONS

MV AGUSTA F4 1000S

Introduced
2004
Engine
In-line
four-cylinder
four-stroke
Capacity
998cc
Power
166bhp
Top speed
187mph

Having designed one of the most stunning motorcycles the world has ever seen in the form of the Ducati 916, Massimo Tamburini could have been forgiven for resting on his laurels. But the Italian genius managed to better even that incredible achievement with his magnificent MV Agusta F4.

Launched in 1999 this machine revived Italy's most glamorous motorcycle marque in fabulous style after a long period of inactivity. A brand new 749cc in-line four-cylinder engine developed with assistance from Ferrari helped to emphasise the thoroughbred pedigree of this two-wheeled beauty, with radial valve technology helping it to give 125bhp and a 170mph top speed.

The figures were healthy, if not world-beating, but what really caused jaws to drop was the incredible attention to detail. The superbly-sculpted tank and quartet of underseat exhaust pipes were instant classics of design, but on closer inspection the motorcycle bristled with top quality components and beautifully subtle style touches featuring the evocative MV logo.

The first version of the F4, the Serie Oro, was a very high specification model with a limited run of 300 built. Dripping with parts manufactured from super light magnesium with a gold finish, including the single-sided swingarm and wheels, this hand-built beauty was offered for sale with the premium price tag of £23,000 ($43,000) in Italy.

The next year saw the introduction of the stock production version of the bike, the F4S, in which the magnesium components of the Serie Oro were replaced with aluminum items.

Then, in 2004, the F4 1000 was introduced, with a larger 998cc capacity engine and largely unaltered styling. The larger engine was good for 166bhp and gave a claimed 187mph top speed.

There have been many limited edition specials including the SPR, Senna and in a tribute to its designer, the Tamburini. This latter version featured ingenious variable-length inlet tracts to boost performance and top speed to 190mph. The most exotic of all is the Veltro, a 177bhp track-only special with a limited run of just 23 bikes.

The MV Agusta F4 1000 remains in production today—and remains one of the world's most desirable motorcycles.

The four exhaust pipes exiting from under the seat are a trademark of every F4. Below is the ultra-exotic Veltro limited edition; the standard F4 1000S is pictured on the left

→ bumpy corner, the 4v's suspension and steering continues to work as normal, giving greater stability.

The extraordinary levels of unique engineering continue throughout the rest of this machine. The U-section frame consists of two machined plates of aircraft-grade aluminum that house the engine. Both front and rear swingarms are constructed from aluminum box sections and combine incredible lightness and strength. The rear shock absorber is another pneumatic unit.

High-tech carbon-fibre is used to construct the air intake and airbox, which also carries the steering head, fairing and front suspension mounts. The titanium exhaust system features header pipes that are different diameters, tuned to suit their lengths.

The overall result is a motorcycle with an incredibly light weight, at 157kg (346lb) dry, and a short 1375mm (54 inch) wheelbase. The whole thing is propelled along by the 150bhp V-twin engine from Ducati's flagship 999R superbike, giving a superb power-to-weight ratio and making for one very fast and responsive motorcycle.

The Vyrus 4v is a technical tour de force, an outstanding machine that is unique and exclusive in the world of motorcycles. Made in very limited numbers, it sells for the princely sum of £38,000 ($71,000). But hey, who said uniqueness and exclusivity ever came cheap?

MOTO GUZZI MGS-01

While the Vyrus 4v challenges conventional ideas of what a motorcycle should look like, other exotic Italian bikes take a more traditional formula and distil it down to its essence to create machines of powerful beauty. One such motorcycle is the Moto Guzzi MGS-01.

Muscular and minimalist, the MGS-01's form reflects Moto Guzzi's heritage and the bike's pure focus as a track-only machine. With design input from renowned Moto Guzzi custom bike specialists Ghezzi and Brian, along with serious mechanical upgrades compared to standard Guzzi machines, →

MOTO GUZZI MGS-01

SPECIFICATIONS

Introduced
2004
Engine
Air-cooled
90° V-twin
four-stroke
Capacity
1225cc
Power
122bhp
Top speed
N/A

→ the result is a motorcycle with a pure form which reflects its purpose.

The bike is dominated by the exposed across-the-frame 90° V-twin engine that has become Moto Guzzi's hallmark. An enlarged version of the old Daytona's 992cc engine, it has been bored out to 1225cc capacity. Special forged Cosworth pistons plus revised camshafts and fuel injection pump up the power to 122bhp, which is delivered to the rear wheel by Guzzi's traditional shaft drive.

It's not an earth-shatteringly powerful engine, but it looks fabulous, with the twin cylinders bulging out of the sides of the bike like a bodybuilder's pecs.

The elegant bodywork acts as a perfect foil to the beefy power unit, enhancing the bike's clean, clutter-free appearance.

The rectangular-section steel-spine frame is integrated with the fuel tank, and routes fresh air to a carbon-fiber airbox below the seat. Suspension and brake components are all top-quality, with Ohlins forks and single rear shock plus Brembo discs and four-pad radial calipers up front.

The first bikes were delivered in 2004, with customers paying £12,500 ($23,000) for the privilege of ownership. As befits a truly exotic motorcycle, the MGS-01 has only been produced in very small

**The MGS-01 packs a traditional Moto Guzzi
V-twin in a beautifully minimalist package**

numbers. A street-legal version is still a possibility; the fact that it has so far failed to materialise just serves to add to the mystique of the MGS-01.

HESKETH V1000

The Hesketh V1000 is a completely different animal to the MGS-01, but in its own way it is just as exotic. With an aristocratic pedigree and a history which dates back to the early 1980s, it is a decidedly 'old school' motorcycle which continues to be built in the heart of England.

This machine was the brainchild of the English Lord Hesketh, who had led his privateer Formula One car racing team to victory with James Hunt at the wheel. Hesketh wanted to use the facilities and expertise built up through this F1 experience to produce a high-quality English motorcycle. Original development took place on Lord Hesketh's estate,

Easton Neston in Northamptonshire, although the first production models were built in a factory in nearby Daventry from 1981.

Weighing in at 550lb (250kg) and with its 992cc V-twin engine producing only 82bhp, outright acceleration was never the V1000's forté. It was designed as a well-appointed grand tourer with the emphasis on covering big mileages in comfort. Top quality Marzocchi suspension was fitted to make progress on the road as unruffled as possible.

Hesketh motorcycles have only ever been built in extremely low volumes, with a mere trickle of these eccentric English machines continuing to find buyers to this day.

This extremely low level of production will inevitably lead to the marque's demise, although the machine has gradually evolved over nearly 25 years of existence, with a recent 1200cc version being ➔

HESKETH V1000

SPECIFICATIONS

Introduced
1981
Engine
Aircooled
90° V-twin
four-stroke
Capacity
992cc
Power
82bhp
Top speed
120mph

The Hesketh V1000 is an old-school motorcycle with an English aristocratic heritage and is still produced today

→ the latest development. The Hesketh V1000 is a rare, endangered and exotic species indeed.

MOTOCZYSZ C1

In total contrast to the quaintly traditional Hesketh V1000, the Motoczysz (pronounced 'Moto-sizz') C1 is as new and radical as you can get. This American-made motorcycle defies convention to such a degree that it is currently the subject of some 15 worldwide patent applications.

The brainchild of famous American architect Michael Czysz, every element of the C1 has been designed from scratch, with ground-breaking technology featured throughout. Even the 990cc 'Z-Line4' engine is a complete re-think of how a motorcycle engine should be built. Innovations include two counter rotating crankshafts, with the cylinders arranged in a 'Z', similar to the 'W' shape used by some high-performance automobiles.

Motoczysz took the traditional inline four and nestled the cylinders closer together, to create the 'Z' configuration. Another unique feature is the fact that the engine has three overhead camshafts: a center cam that operates all the intakes, and two half-camshafts that operate the exhaust valves of two cylinders each.

Rather than mounting the engine across the frame, as with conventional in-line four-cylinder layouts, the engine is rotated through 90° so that the crankshafts run along the axis of the wheelbase. The counter-rotating crankshafts are designed to eliminate the torque effect which will normally rock a bike with a crankshaft in line with the wheels from side to side. By cancelling out this effect, the aim is to greatly improve the bike's handling characteristics.

The front end is designed to allow more high-pressure air to pass through the bodywork and use it to feed the airbox and under-tail radiator, instead of moving it around the outside of the bike. The front suspension is similarly avant-garde in its design, with Motoczysz's unique '6X-Flex' system dispensing with conventional twin hydraulic forks and using sliders

bolted to oxagonal stanchions. The system is designed to reduce lateral flex and increase traction during cornering. Front suspension is dealt with by an Ohlins monoshock positioned within the headstock.

The rest of the C1 also reflects Czysz's creative thinking. The engine is mounted in a high-tech carbon-fiber deltabox frame, with rear suspension dealt with by an Ohlins monoshock unit with a linkage that can be adjusted independently from the spring rate, allowing for greater fine-tuning.

Everything is designed to be easily adjustable and accessible, reflecting Czysz's experience as a racer and his desire to produce a machine whose set-up can be quickly fine-tuned in the frantic atmosphere of the pit lane. The whole gearbox, for instance, can be removed, the ratios changed, and the gearbox replaced in a super-quick 10 minutes.

To emphasise the race-focused nature of this project, the C1 was launched at the American round of the MotoGP championship at Laguna Seca, →

PHOTOGRAPHY: TOM FRISCH

MOTOCZYSZ C1

Introduced
2006
Engine
Liquid-cooled 'Z-Line 4' four-stroke
Capacity
998cc
Power
220bhp (estimated)
Top speed
200mph (estimated)

The Motoczysz C1 is a completely original design and is the most expensive production bike in the world at $100,000

KTM RC8

Sharp and radical, KTM's new superbike is on the verge of making it into production. Bring it on...

KTM surprised everyone at the Tokyo Motorcycle Show in 2003 by unveiling a concept superbike called the RC8.

KTM had never previously been a player in the superbike game, the Austrian firm had gained its considerable reputation through great success in off-road competitions such as world championship-level motocross and enduro racing.

Add in the RC8's sheer angular aggressiveness, all painted up in KTM's traditional vibrant orange, and the result was a shock package that shook up preconceived notions of what a superbike should look like.

The world of motorcycles has seen many such concept bikes come and go. Most of them are mere promotional items or notional exercises with no hope of making it into series production. A very few end up being developed into production models, although usually in a very watered-down form compared to the original show concept.

KTM's RC8 bucks that trend, however, because the company is continuing to develop the bike with a view to putting it on sale to the public in 2007. Not only that, the latest development machine looks almost identical to the startling original concept model shown on these pages.

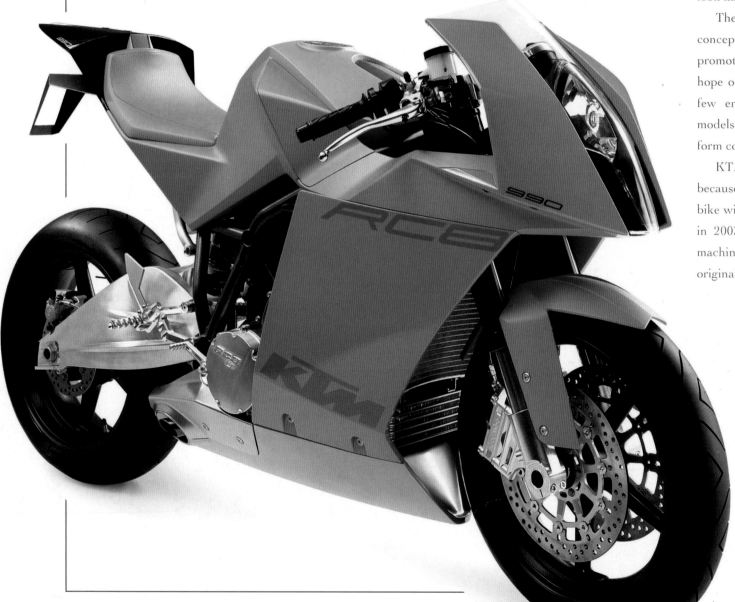

KTM is looking to follow up its Super Duke with another radical looking street bike. This is the concept version of the RC8; production version will look very similar

PHOTOGRAPHY: H MITTERBAUER

Powered by a version of the company's own 990cc V-twin engine with capacity enlarged to 1150cc, the RC8 should make at least 170bhp, giving a 175mph-plus top speed potential.

The KTM's tubular steel frame, superbly crafted aluminum swingarm and exhaust muffler underslung beneath the engine should add up to a very light package, with the weight well centralised within the chassis to give the machine fine balance and handling characteristics.

Designed as a street-legal machine, the RC8 may be coming your way sooner than you'd think...

KTM RC8

SPECIFICATIONS

Introduced
2007 (planned)
Engine
Water-cooled
75° V-twin
four-stroke
Capacity
1150cc
Power
170bhp (estimated)
Top speed
175mph (estimated)

→ California in July 2006. A race program is planned by the company, with the possibility of 'wild card' one-off entries in various race series in 2007.

Production plans for the C1 elevate it to the highest level of exotica. The initial limited run of 50 race bikes is being offered for $100,000 (£53,000), aimed at rich track-day fiends and collectors, making it the most expensive production motorcycle in the world at the time this book went to print.

The company's future plans include the production of various models ranging in price from $20,000 up to $100,000 (£10,700-53,000) in the period up until 2011.

The Motoczysz C1 is a radical and remarkable American motorcycle in every respect. A testament to the creativity and originality of its creator's design skills, it has all the hallmarks of a machine that could force motorcycle manufacturers into a complete re-think of their concepts of bike construction.

It will certainly influence the construction of future race bikes, and as technology that is developed and proven on the race track often percolates down to street-legal machines, some of Michael Czysz's innovations may well help to improve the dynamics and performance of the motorcycles that everyday bikers ride on the road someday.

MORE RADICAL AMERICAN DESIGN

Confederate is another American motorcycle manufacturer that takes an unconventional approach to bike design and construction. Founded in 1991 in San Francisco, California, with the aim of creating unique American motorcycles, it moved to New Orleans, Louisiana in 1993 and produced its first model in 1994.

The devastating Hurricane Katrina of 2005 caused severe damage to the company's factory, and production was moved to Birmingham, Alabama, where it resumed in 2006. Although it is a very small company, employing only 12 people at the start of 2006, Confederate's bikes and their radically cool image have attracted some serious celebrity →

CONFEDERATE HELLCAT

SPECIFICATIONS

Introduced
1994
Engine
Air-cooled
45° V-twin
four-stroke
Capacity
124 cu in (2032cc)
Power
140bhp
Top speed
N/A

→ endorsement, with owners including film star Brad Pitt. Fellow actor Tom Cruise also rode into New York City on one of Confederate's first Birmingham-made bikes for the premiere of the film Mission Impossible III in May, 2006.

CONFEDERATE HELLCAT

It took Confederate's owner, Matt Chambers 13 years of work to produce the Hellcat. The machine you see below is the result of all that toil and effort, and it's one of the wildest-looking two-wheelers you will ever see.

A true original, this machine is painstakingly hand-built with the aim of achieving the ultimate in quality workmanship. The Hellcat's stripped-down, aggressive styling leaves the component parts of the bike on full show, allowing onlookers to drool over the custom-crafted parts of this American rebel—if they dare to get close enough!

Despite its radical looks, this machine has a traditional heart, being powered by a good old American V-twin built by S&S and displacing 124 cubic inches (2032cc). With 140bhp to propel 530lb (240kg) of motorcycle along, the engine gives the Hellcat the performance to match its looks.

In an ingenious and unique design feature, the header pipes meet at a flexible junction, from whence the swingarm acts as the rear part of the exhaust pipe! The gas tank is constructed in superbly sculpted carbon-fiber, with Confederate's distinctive

The Hellcat's uniquely rebellious style and superbly crafted components have attracted Hollywood movie stars to its list of well-heeled owners

solo saddle built from the same high-tech material. The eclectic mix of styles is completed by the huge, cruiser-style eight-inch-wide rear wheel and streetfighter-esque triple stacked headlights.

Such pure individuality comes at a price which reflects the exclusivity of owning a Hellcat—only 500 of the original model were made, and the latest F131 model featured here will have a production run limited to a mere 150 bikes. To own one of these beautifully-executed pieces of rebellious engineering requires parting with $60,000 (£32,000)

CONFEDERATE WRAITH

Nothing can quite prepare you for your first sight of the Confederate Wraith. Constructed to the same uncompromising standards and complete disregard for convention as the Hellcat, it is a creation guaranteed to stop even the most jaded biker dead in his tracks.

The arc of the bike's tubular spine is one of its most striking features, and it forms a practical purpose as well as making a dramatic visual statement as its rear end holds the hidden rear suspension. It is constructed from carbon-fiber, the lightweight, high-tech material that also forms the girder fork which acts as part of the bike's front suspension.

The single-sided aluminum swingarm conspires with the hidden rear suspension to enhance the Wraith's clean, uncluttered look, as does the gas tank, which is underslung beneath the engine. →

CONFEDERATE WRAITH

SPECIFICATIONS

Introduced
2006 (planned)
Engine
Air-cooled
45° V-twin
four-stroke
Capacity
100 cu in (1640cc)
Power
125bhp (estimated)
Top speed
130mph

Even more radical than the Hellcat, the Wraith is unlike any other motorcycle you have seen before. It is a true one–off that will be built in extremely limited numbers

Exotic Hondas: the RC30 (above) and RC45 (below) were street-legal versions of successful race bikes

→ And that all-American power unit is proudly displayed for all to see. An air-cooled V-twin of 100 cubic inch (1640cc) capacity, it delivers 125bhp to thrust 415lb of motorcycle along the highway,

Nearing the final prototype stage as this book went to press, Confederate aims to produce the Wraith in similarly limited numbers to the Hellcat, with a sticker price of $55,000 (£30,000). And if any prospective owners are not used to drawing a crowd, they'd better get used to the idea before taking their Wraith out on the street!

JAPANESE EXOTICA

The mass-produced products of the Japanese motorcycle industry may seem a world away from the radical creations of Confederate and Motoczysz, but the Land of the Rising Sun has given birth to its own particular brand of exotic motorcycles. One of the most famous is the Honda RC30 which arrived in 1987, born of the pursuit of excellence.

HONDA RC30

According to popular legend, the RC30 was the product of Soichiro Honda's desire to show the world that his company could build the ultimate sports bike. A no-expense-spared, no-compromise machine, it was designed to stamp Honda's authority by being the best on the street as well as on the race track in the fledgling World Superbike series.

As a production-based series, World Superbike rules stipulated that a specified number of street-legal versions of a particular model must be sold to allow the corresponding race bike to compete, a process called 'homologation'.

The RC30 got off to a flying start after its introduction, winning the first two World Superbike championships and went from strength to strength, smashing records at the infamously tough Isle of Man TT races in the UK in the process.

The bike was hand-built and powered by a tuned version of Honda's 748cc V4 RVF engine giving 112bhp and wrapped in a huge twin-beam aluminum frame. This labour-intensive endeavour produced a price that was shocking for a Japanese motorcycle of the day, or any other type of motorcycle for that matter. The RC30 cost a breath-taking £8495 ($16,000) in the UK when it was first released, and still fetches big money today. Nearly two decades since it was last built, it retains an exotic allure which makes it a true icon.

HONDA RC45

The successor to the all-conquering RC30, the RC45 was another 'homologation special', with a limited production run of its street-legal variant introduced in 1994, enabling it to take part in superbike racing.

Like its predecessor, it was powered by a V4 four-stroke engine and had a single-sided swingarm, although the RC45's engine was fed by fuel injection rather than carburettors. The frame was also revised to give a lower centre of gravity and to allow a larger airbox which pressurized the air before it entered the fuel injection system.

Capable of over 150bhp when fitted with the optional Honda race kit, the 749cc RC45 was a serious performer and continued the successful racing heritage of the RC30.

With a price tag of $27,000 in the USA (£14,500), the RC45 was even more outrageously expensive than the RC30, which is another reason why it was and remains a rarely-spotted machine on the road.

YAMAHA R7

The R7 was Yamaha's take on the 'homologation special', and is one of the rarest production bikes ever to come out of a Japanese factory, with only 500 built. In order to buy one, you first needed to prove to Yamaha that you were committed to a full season's racing (or were at least sponsoring a racer for a season), making it a very exclusive machine indeed with a premium price of £20,000 ($32,000) to match.

Powered by a 749cc in-line four-cylinder engine, it produced 105bhp in street-legal form. With an ➔

Yamaha's R7 is one of the rarest bikes ever to emerge from a Japanese factory

SPECIFICATIONS

HONDA RC30

Introduced
1987
Engine
Liquid-cooled
90° V4
four-stroke
Capacity
748cc
Power
112bhp
Top speed
150mph

SPECIFICATIONS

HONDA RC45

Introduced
1994
Engine
Liquid-cooled
90° V4
four-stroke
Capacity
749cc
Power
120bhp
Top speed
160mph

SPECIFICATIONS

YAMAHA R7

Introduced
1999
Engine
In-line
four-cylinder
four-stroke
Capacity
749cc
Power
135bhp
Top speed
174mph

→ adjustment to the electronic fuel injection system, a race pipe and a few other modifications, the R7 could be tuned to 135bhp, with full race versions hitting around 150bhp.

Renowned for its great combination of power and superb handling, the R7 remains one of the most desirable Japanese sports motorcycles ever.

LAZARETH: THE FRENCH CONNECTION

Lazareth has built a reputation as one of the most flamboyant special motorcycle builders currently in operation. The French firm, based in Annecy at the foot of the European Alps, takes components from existing production motorcycles and adds its own innovative and often outrageous influence to create machines which are eye-poppingly radical.

One such machine is the Dokujya, pictured left. It may be powered by the 996cc V-twin engine from Honda's VTR1000, but apart from that it bears no relation whatsoever to that particular Japanese

mass-produced motorcycle. For starters, Lazareth bolt on the supercharger from the Mini Cooper car to boost power to 140bhp.

A specially-fabricated aluminum subframe is fixed to the top of the engine and carries the custom-made tank, handlebars, fairing and seat unit plus the aluminum single-sided fork leg. Front suspension is by a single shock absorber which runs up inside the central tube. At the rear, the swingarm is a modified MV Agusta F4 unit, with twin exhaust pipes exiting from underneath a customised tail unit from a Yamaha R1 and being slash-cut so that they finish flush with the bodywork.

Like all Lazareth's creations, the Dokujya (which is Japanese for snake venom) is built to customer order—and customers needs to be as outrageous as the bike itself to justify ownership. Not only that, with a purchase price in the region of £25,000 ($46,800), they will also have to have an outrageous amount of disposable income! →

LAZARETH DOKUJYA

SPECIFICATIONS

Introduced
2006
Engine
Liquid-cooled
90° V-twin
four-stroke
Capacity
996cc
Power
140bhp (estimated)
Top speed
N/A

" **Lazareth is one of the most flamboyant special motorcycle builders in operation** "

Lazareth's Dokujya (far left) is the wildest Honda-powered motorcycle you will ever see. The company also builds other specials like the Yamaha-based 1000 GTS (left)

Ducati

This street-legal MotoGP machine is the ultimate motorcycle for any racing fan's fantasy garage

DESMOSEDICI RR

The Desmosedici RR has caused a mad scramble amongst buyers keen to get hold of the first ever street–legal MotoGP bike

This has to be the ultimate of all ultimate motorcycles. Ducati's Desmosedici RR is not just another 'race bike for the road', it is a street-legal version of the company's MotoGP race bike—a bike which has a proven record as a race winner in what is the world's top road racing championship. Pedigrees simply don't come any more impressive than that.

Rumours that the famous Italian company were working towards producing the world's first MotoGP bike for the road had been rife throughout the industry for a long time, and after a two-year development period the finished model was finally unveiled in a ceremony at Italy's equally famous Mugello race track in June 2006.

Although customers will have to wait until 2007 for the first Desmosedici RRs to be delivered, the machine's full specification was revealed at its

launch. It is powered by an engine with the same layout and capacity dimensions as the Desmosedici MotoGP bike, a 989cc V4, with the ability to produce 205bhp—that's 40bhp less than the race bike, but still enough to blow any other production bike off the road.

As a road-legal machine, the RR conforms to emissions and noise regulations, but Ducati will provide a race kit with each bike sold, which will include a straight-through exhaust and a more track-focused electronics package. The bike's full power potential of 205bhp will be unleashed when this kit is fitted.

Other technical highlights of the bike include the first self-supporting, carbon-fibre one-piece tail unit ever fitted to a road bike, through which the

twin exhausts pipes exit upwards, plus specially-produced Bridgestone tires that are designed specifically for the Desmosedici RR.

High-tech Ohlins gas-pressurised forks are fitted to provide suspension at the front, with monobloc Brembo brake calipers and brake discs that were designed for the Ducati MotoGP bike providing the stopping power.

Marchesini wheels made from superlight magnesium along with MotoGP-style bodywork with added headlights and rear lights complete the mouth-watering package.

Ducati says the Desmosedici RR is as close to the MotoGP bike as they could possibly make it in street-legal form. It certainly looks the part, whether in its traditional Ducati all-red paintwork or in the alternative white-striped colourscheme based on the race bike's livery.

Both versions will come with a full replica MotoGP sticker kit to give the bike the fully authentic look and to allow owners the chance to live out their racing fantasies to the full.

The Desmosedici RR is one of the most eagerly awaited machines in the history of motorcycling, and as this book went to press, hopeful buyers were scrambling to get down their deposits against its £37,500 ($70,000) price tag.

Some prospective buyers are prepared to buy one of Ducati's 999R superbikes just because this will get them higher up the queue for a Desmosedici RR. Ducati is even considering setting up a second production line to meet the demand.

DUCATI DESMOSEDICI RR

SPECIFICATIONS

Introduced
2007 (planned)
Engine
Water-cooled
90° V4
four-stroke
Capacity
989cc
Power
205bhp
Top speed
N/A

Japanese tire company Bridgestone, which manufactures the tires for Ducati's MotoGP bikes, have developed a special tire solely for the Desmosedici RR

Harley-Davidson
Softail Springer

Harley-Davidson
    Night Rod Special

Arlen Ness:
    Untouchable
    Peter Max Bike
    Two Bad
    Ness-tique
    Strictly Business
    Blower Bike
    Ness Café
    Ferrari Bike
    Ness-stalgia
    Aluminum OHC Evo
    Convertible Sled
    Arrow Bike
    Top Banana
    Half and Half
    Smooth-Ness

Victory Kingpin

Victory Hammer

Victory Vegas Jackpot

Ducati T-Bob Special

TRIUMPH AMERICA

BMW R1200C

Triumph America

Kawasaki VN2000

Yamaha Midnight Star

Honda Rune

Suzuki Intruder M1800R

Boss Hoss

Triumph Rocket III

CRUISERS & CUSTOM *Motorcycles*

Born in the USA, the cruiser is a type of bike that suits the American landscape perfectly. The traditional cruiser's laid-back style makes it a perfect companion when you're riding all day on endless interstate highways. Custom motorcycles are a uniquely self-expressive extension of the cruiser style

The wide open spaces of the USA have become a worldwide symbol of the epic journey, with its widescreen landscape serving as the inspiration for countless road movies. Travelling on endless highways through some of the most spectacular scenery on the planet has become part of the American dream, representing the spirit of adventure which helped to build the country.

The sheer scale of the place and the vast distances involved also brought about the birth of a type of motorcycle that is quintessentially American —the cruiser. The basic formula is simple: a relaxed riding position with high handlebars and a big, lazy engine which majors on easy-going, low-revving grunt and allows for maximum relaxation during monumental road trips.

The classic cruiser riding position is legs bent as if you were sitting in an armchair, with a straight back and arms comfortably outstretched forwards. It's a recipe for highway cruising that is ingrained in the fabric of American motorcycle culture. ➔

→ The company which has become synonymous with the American cruiser is Harley-Davidson. Its history is almost as long as the history of the American motorcycle itself, with the first one built way back in 1903. Things have come a long way since then, but the company still majors on its heritage and builds bikes that echo the machines of the past, like the Softail Springer.

HARLEY-DAVIDSON SOFTAIL SPRINGER

The big, rumbling engine is a Harley-Davidson hallmark, and even after decades of evolution its configuration remains the same: a V-twin with the cylinders arranged at a 45° angle. The company's current Softail Springer model also harks back to the olden days with its suspension systems: the 'Softail' rear end and 'Springer' front end. Both are designed to emulate the look of period Harleys while offering more modern suspension performance.

The Softail is a cantilever suspension system with two shock absorbers hidden out of sight under the engine to give the uncluttered look of the 'hardtail' Harleys produced before the introduction of rear suspension.

Springer forks are designed to evoke the visual effect of the girder forks that were the state of →

SPECIFICATIONS

HARLEY-DAVIDSON SOFTAIL SPRINGER

Introduced
2006
Engine
Air-cooled
45° V-twin
four-stroke
Capacity
96 cu in (1584cc)
Power
N/A
Top speed
N/A

Harley-Davidson's Softail Springer gets the most extreme of the company's 'retro-tech' features: Springer front suspension, a modern interpretation of the girder forks of the 1940s

→ the art in the 1940s, with the benefit of computer-aided design and improved functionality to appease modern-day bikers who are used to today's more sophisticated level of suspension performance.

This idea of using the classic style of components from earlier eras, applying modern engineering and production techniques and adding a modern styling twist has been dubbed 'Retro Tech', and has become a cornerstone of Harley design. Harley's styling guru Willie G Davidson has his own take on this, dubbing the concept 'New Nostalgia'

With the Softail Springer, Harley-Davidson enthusiasts can buy a motorcycle with a combination of old-style Harley looks with a more contemporary riding experience. However, as usual with Harley-Davidson you have to pay handsomely for the experience, with prices starting at $17,000 (£13,195 in the UK).

HARLEY–DAVIDSON NIGHT ROD SPECIAL

For those who aren't turned on by the traditional cruiser and just want the baddest Harley on the block, there is only one choice—the Night Rod Special. As mean-looking as a WWF wrestler and a hell of a lot sexier, this is the evil brother of the ground-breaking V-Rod, and is new for 2007.

The V-Rod broke the Harley mould in 2002, with its liquid-cooled VRSC engine and all-round dynamics that were a big improvement on any of the company's previous models. For the Harley faithful who had been brought up on chugging cruisers with air-cooled engines, it was hard to swallow, but at least there was still plenty of chrome to polish.

The Night Rod Special bins virtually all of that shiny stuff in favour of a cool gloss-and-satin colour scheme, giving a superbly stealthy look. Even the engine is 'blacked-out' and the bike sits 3/4-inch (20mm) lower than the standard V-Rod, with a fat 43/4-inch inch (120mm) section rear tyre

As black as the ace of spades apart from its chrome forks, satin-finished exhaust pipes and orange-pinstriped wheels, this machine rocks like

no other Harley has rocked before. And not just in terms of its looks.

This bike is more hot rod than cruiser, with its 69 cubic inch (1130cc) engine giving neck-straining acceleration up to around 130mph despite the bike's considerable weight at 643lbs (292kg).

The engine is a 60° V-twin rather than the classic 45° configuration, and is also also untypical for a Harley-Davidson in that it is tuned for high revs rather than low-down grunt, although it will happily cruise smoothly at low speed if you want it to.

And boy, it looks cool doing it. The Night Rod Special is a motorcycle → CONTINUED ON PAGE 49

HARLEY–DAVIDSON NIGHT ROD SPECIAL

SPECIFICATIONS

Introduced	2006
Engine	Liquid-cooled 60° V-twin four-stroke
Capacity	1130cc
Power	110bhp
Top speed	130mph

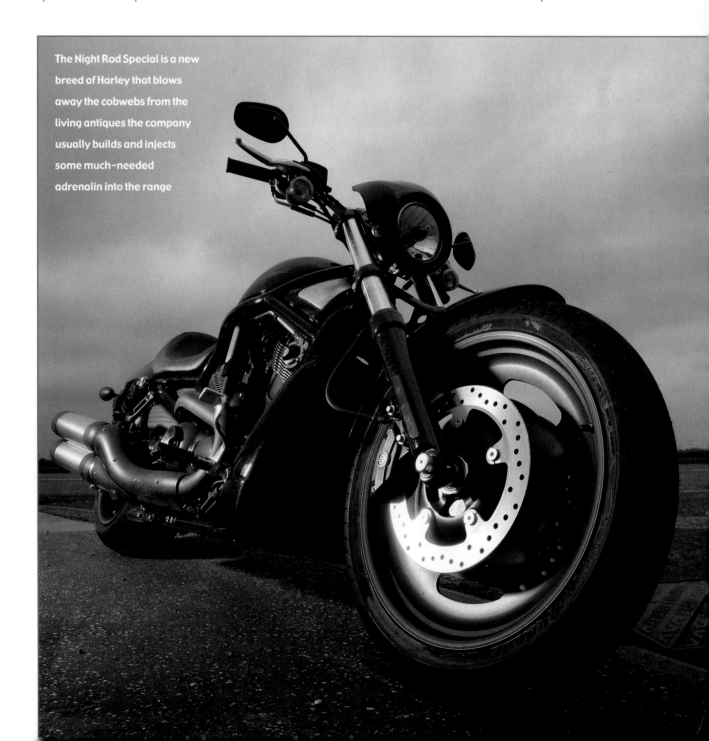

The Night Rod Special is a new breed of Harley that blows away the cobwebs from the living antiques the company usually builds and injects some much-needed adrenalin into the range

Arlen Ness

Prepare to be astounded by this selection of incredible creations from the Grand Master of custom motorcyles...

Arlen Ness is known as a quiet, unassuming kind of guy. Which is weird, because the machines he builds are quite the opposite. Quite simply, they are some of the most outrageous, creative and downright beautiful motorcycles ever built, as you will discover as you feast your eyes on a selection of them over the next 10 pages of this book.

His portfolio of amazing creations spans four decades, each one a rolling sculpture crafted with incredible care and attention to detail by Ness and his band of fellow craftsmen. The Arlen Ness brand is now a huge worldwide business concern, with its

Untouchable is based on a bike Ness bought for $300. It was rebuilt over and over, gradually reaching the state below over 14 years

UNTOUCHABLE

Built 1963-1977 **Engine** 1947 Harley-Davidson Knucklehead enlarged to 100 cu in (1640cc), Magnuson supercharger, twin Weber carburetors

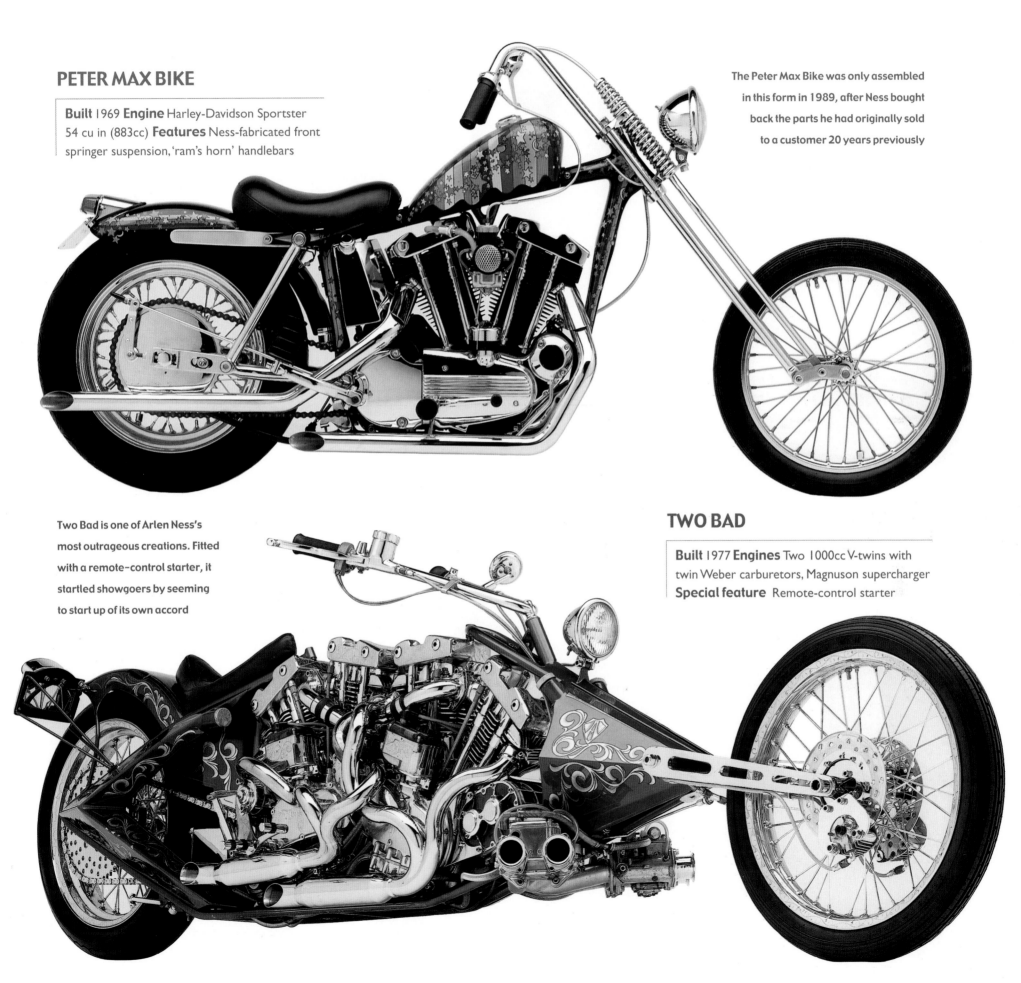

PETER MAX BIKE

Built 1969 **Engine** Harley-Davidson Sportster 54 cu in (883cc) **Features** Ness-fabricated front springer suspension, 'ram's horn' handlebars

The Peter Max Bike was only assembled in this form in 1989, after Ness bought back the parts he had originally sold to a customer 20 years previously

Two Bad is one of Arlen Ness's most outrageous creations. Fitted with a remote-control starter, it startled showgoers by seeming to start up of its own accord

TWO BAD

Built 1977 **Engines** Two 1000cc V-twins with twin Weber carburetors, Magnuson supercharger **Special feature** Remote-control starter

NESS-TIQUE

Built 1978 **Engine** Harley-Davidson V-twin, fins removed from bottom of barrels **Frame** Small diameter chrome-molybdenum 5/8-inch tubing

Ness-Tique's 'antique custom' look was inspired by a trophy that Ness won, a replica of the first ever Harley-Davidson

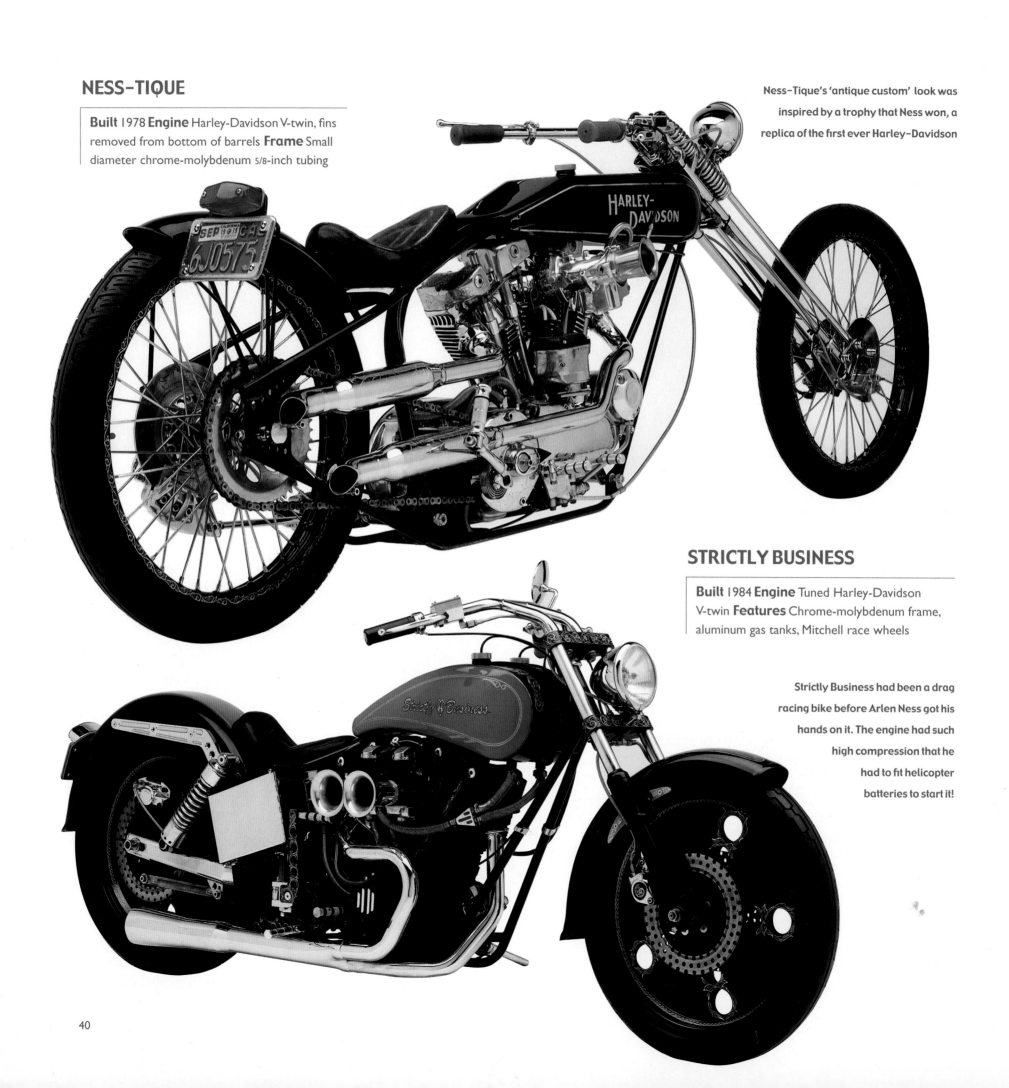

STRICTLY BUSINESS

Built 1984 **Engine** Tuned Harley-Davidson V-twin **Features** Chrome-molybdenum frame, aluminum gas tanks, Mitchell race wheels

Strictly Business had been a drag racing bike before Arlen Ness got his hands on it. The engine had such high compression that he had to fit helicopter batteries to start it!

70,000-square-foot headquarters in Dublin, California dealing in everything from motorcycles to custom components, clothing and even toys—mostly wearing the Arlen Ness brand.

It's the result of 40 years of hard work and perseverance from the guy who is now justifiably dubbed an 'American Legend', but the Arlen Ness empire has grown from very humble beginnings.

His first motorcycle was a 1947 Harley-Davidson Knucklehead bought for $300 in 1963. Over the next 14 years, Ness used the bike as a test bed for his customising techniques, as well as his daily ride. Rebuilding the bike nearly every year, creating new styles and looks and developing his skills and techniques in the creation of custom bikes and paint jobs, he gradually built up a reputation as an artisan and an innovator in the world of individualized motorcycles.

Ness finally stopped reworking and re-inventing that motorcycle, which came to be known as 'Untouchable' (see p38) in 1977. By then, he had made a name for himself as a skilled painter of

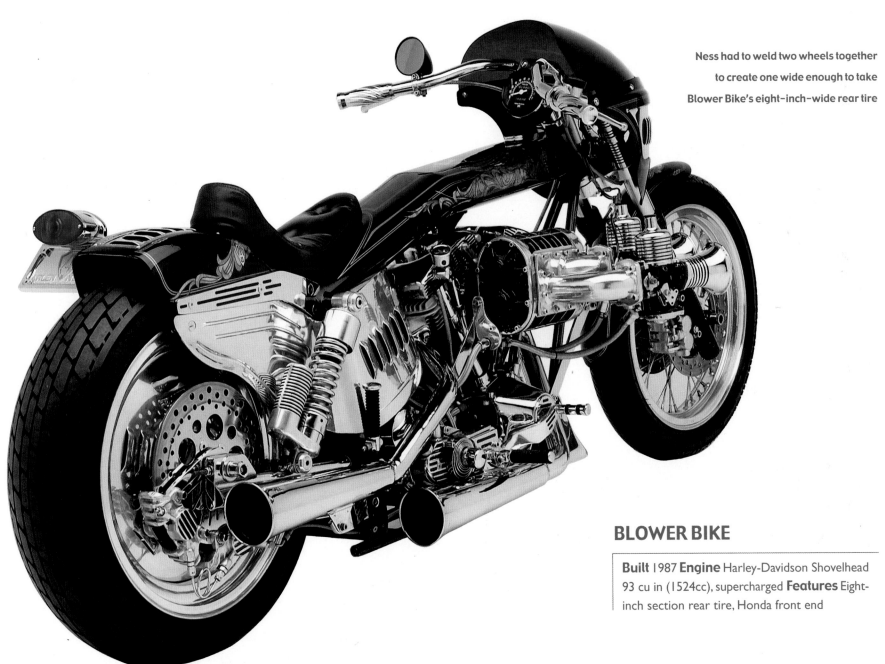

Ness had to weld two wheels together to create one wide enough to take Blower Bike's eight-inch-wide rear tire

BLOWER BIKE

Built 1987 **Engine** Harley-Davidson Shovelhead 93 cu in (1524cc), supercharged **Features** Eight-inch section rear tire, Honda front end

custom paint jobs for other people's bikes and had started up his own accessories shop. In the process, he had established contacts with fellow craftsmen who could help him express his creative drive to build his own unique motorcycles from scratch.

Over the next three decades, the bikes that Arlen Ness built set the trends and fashions for the custom motorcycle scene, breaking new ground in terms of design and style as he went.

One of his most outrageous creations ever was put together in 1977, being first shown at the Oakland Roadster Show of that year. It's hardly surprising that he needed to draft in friends to get some last-minute help to finish the bike when you consider what Ness had thrown at it.

The bike had not one, but two V-twin engines, giving a total capacity of 2000cc. But that wasn't enough. Ness bolted on a Magnusson supercharger and two huge Weber carburetors with their bellmouth intakes gasping for air on either side below the front of the engine. Torsion-bar suspension and hub-center steering made the front wheel look as if it was floating ahead of the main body of the bike, which was incredibly low and long.

The overkill went on, with two batteries, four gas tanks, an incredible paint job featuring gold leaf and

Arlen Ness acquired the bike that formed the basis of Ness Café from Canada. He bought it as a wreck, then set about customizing it

NESS CAFÉ

Built 1990 **Based on** Harley-Davidson XR1000 Sportster **Modifications** Extended swingarm, increased rake, fairing, aluminum bodywork

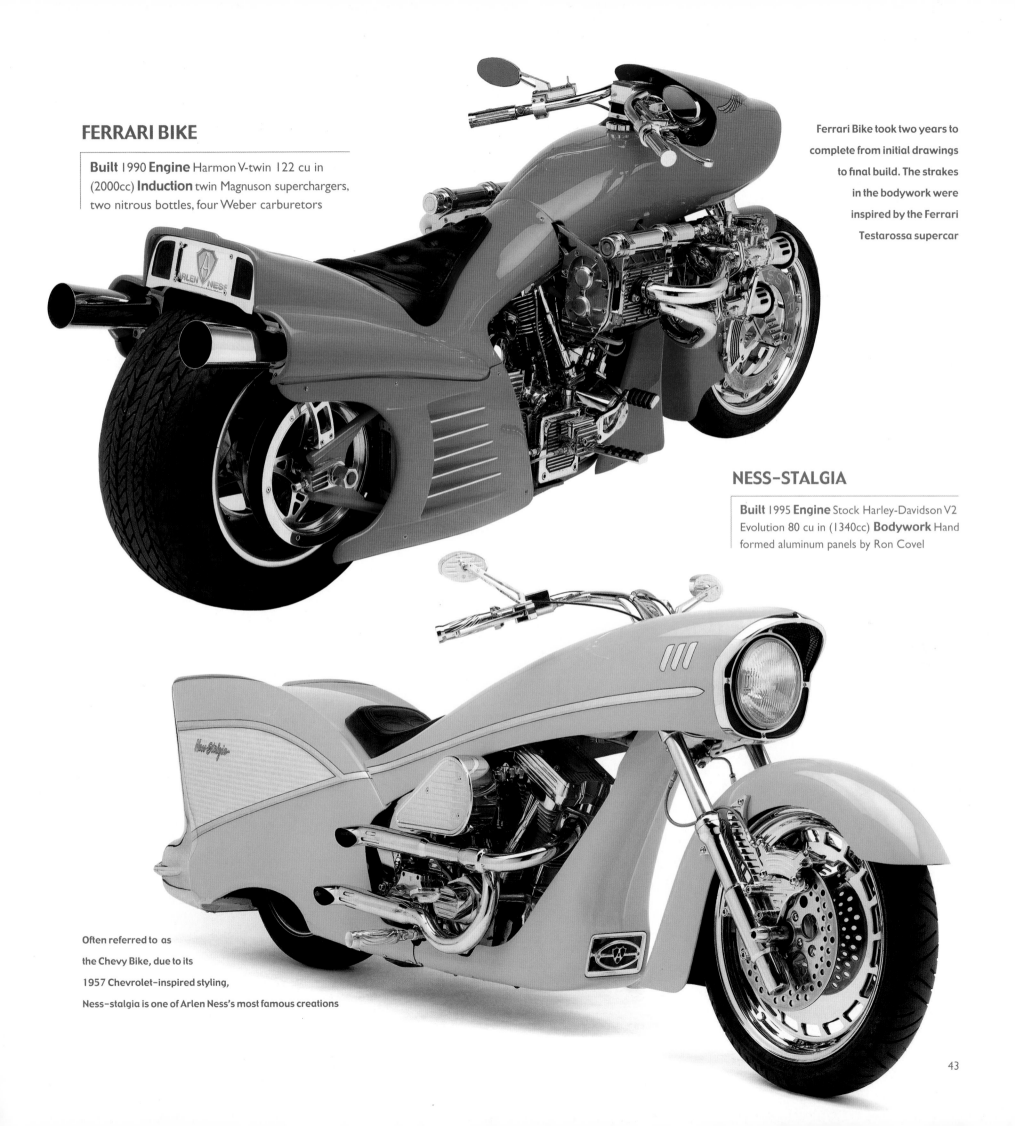

FERRARI BIKE

Built 1990 **Engine** Harmon V-twin 122 cu in (2000cc) **Induction** twin Magnuson superchargers, two nitrous bottles, four Weber carburetors

Ferrari Bike took two years to complete from initial drawings to final build. The strakes in the bodywork were inspired by the Ferrari Testarossa supercar

NESS–STALGIA

Built 1995 **Engine** Stock Harley-Davidson V2 Evolution 80 cu in (1340cc) **Bodywork** Hand formed aluminum panels by Ron Covel

Often referred to as the Chevy Bike, due to its 1957 Chevrolet-inspired styling, Ness-stalgia is one of Arlen Ness's most famous creations

an obsessive attention to detail. Two Bad (see p39) won the show, with Ness receiving a $10,000 Cartier trophy—a gold and silver replica of the first ever Harley-Davidson motorcycle.

This trophy proved to be the inspiration for another of Arlen Ness's most celebrated bikes, Ness-tique (see page 40). He was so impressed with the trophy, he determined to build a custom bike with an antique theme, something very light and very different. Ness-tique was to set a trend

for minimalist, stripped-down antique-style bikes, with its frame made from small-diameter 5/8-inch chrome-moly tubing, giving a particularly light and airy feel to the whole thing.

To add to the stripped-down look, the lower fins were cut from the bottom of the engine barrels, as was the bottom cover of the kick-start mechanism, and the most minimal seat possible was used.

Probably the most beautiful motorcycle Arlen Ness has ever made was built in 1995. Smooth-Ness

ALUMINUM OHC EVO

Built 1998 **Engine** Arlen Ness overhead camshaft 100 cu in (1639cc) V-twin designed by Pete Ardema **Frame** Special aluminum lightweight construction weighing 17lb (7.7kg)

Aluminum plays a big part in this bike, with the frame, pipes, mufflers and a large part of the engine all made from the lightweight metal

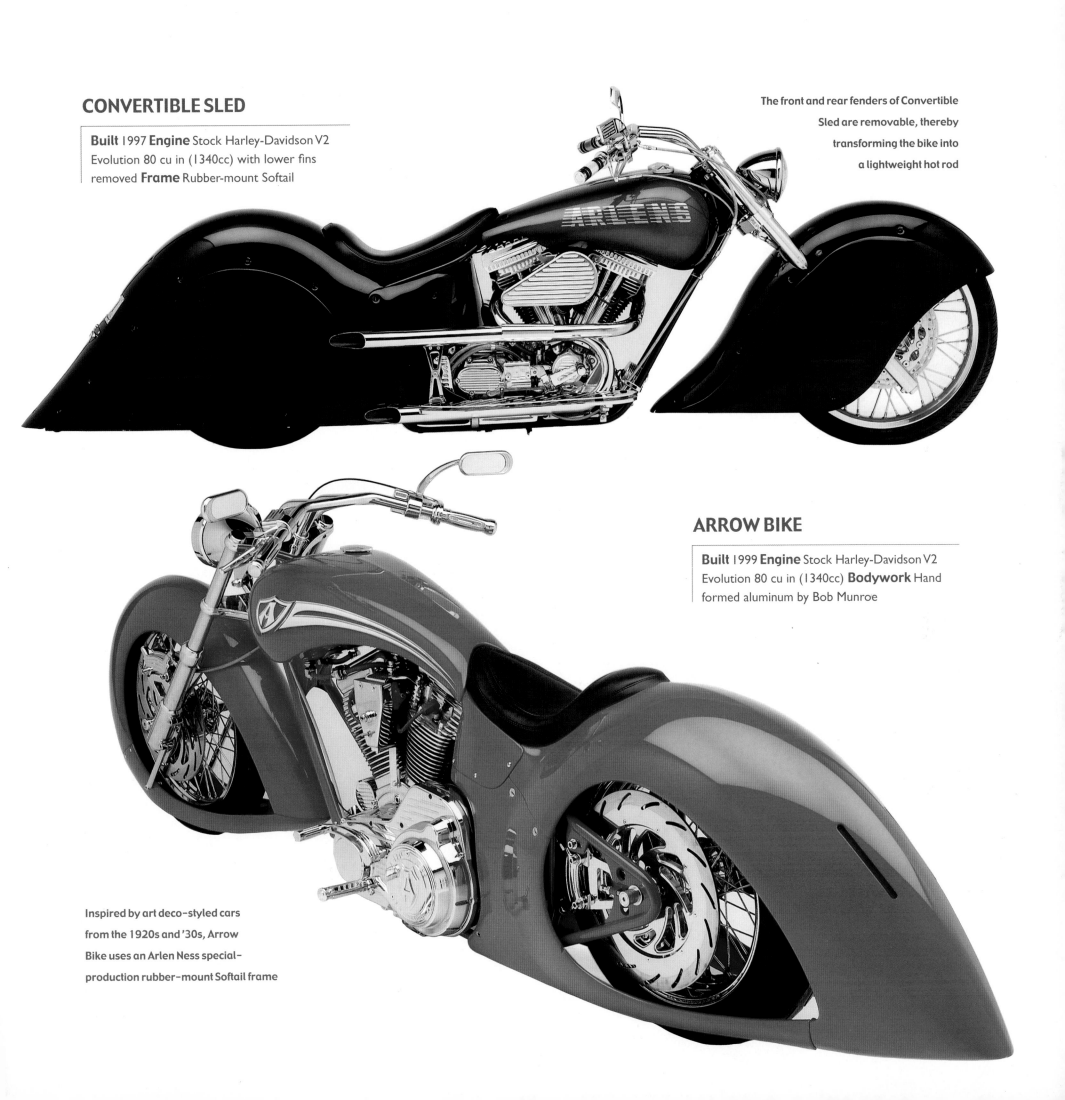

CONVERTIBLE SLED

Built 1997 **Engine** Stock Harley-Davidson V2 Evolution 80 cu in (1340cc) with lower fins removed **Frame** Rubber-mount Softail

The front and rear fenders of Convertible Sled are removable, thereby transforming the bike into a lightweight hot rod

ARROW BIKE

Built 1999 **Engine** Stock Harley-Davidson V2 Evolution 80 cu in (1340cc) **Bodywork** Hand formed aluminum by Bob Munroe

Inspired by art deco–styled cars from the 1920s and '30s, Arrow Bike uses an Arlen Ness special–production rubber-mount Softail frame

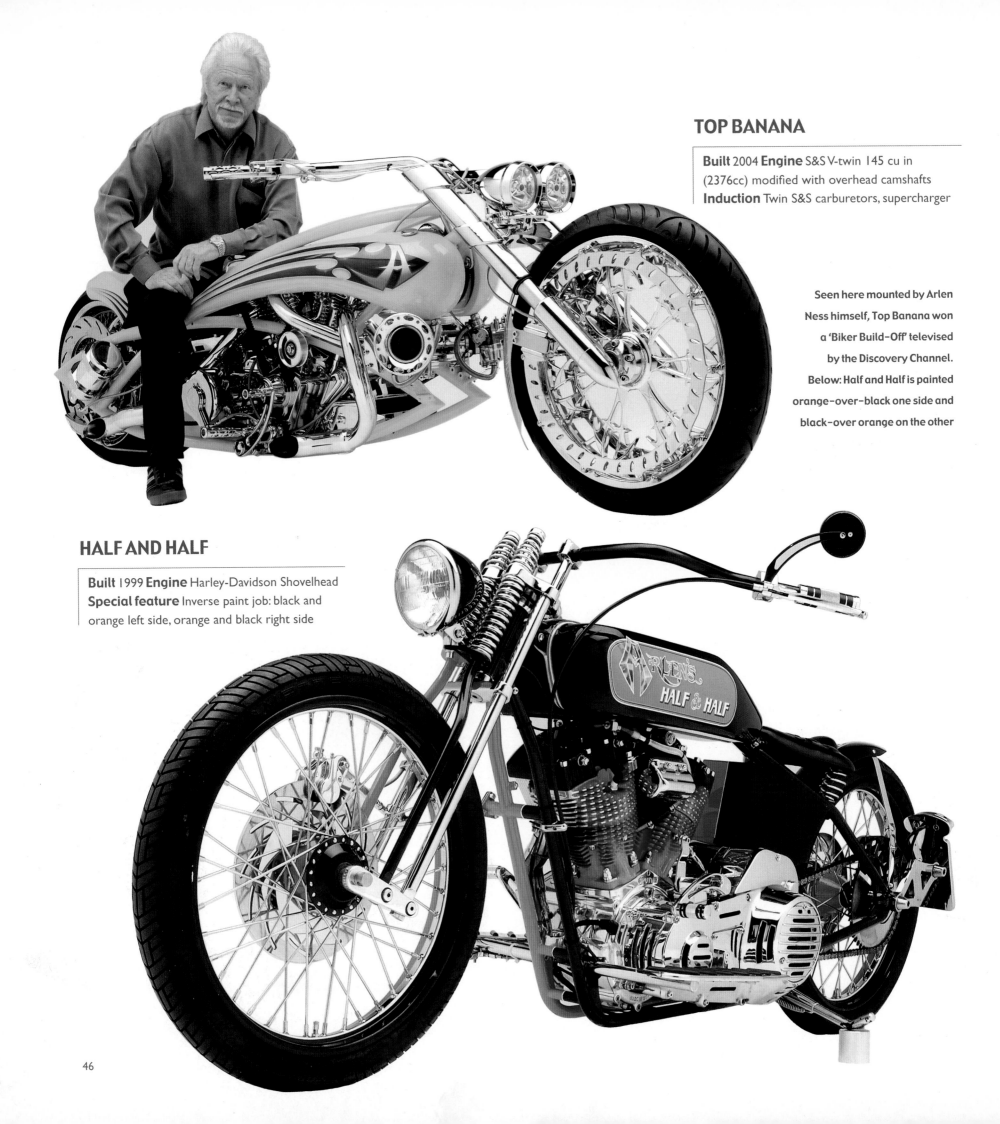

TOP BANANA

Built 2004 **Engine** S&S V-twin 145 cu in (2376cc) modified with overhead camshafts **Induction** Twin S&S carburetors, supercharger

Seen here mounted by Arlen Ness himself, Top Banana won a 'Biker Build-Off' televised by the Discovery Channel. Below: Half and Half is painted orange-over-black one side and black-over orange on the other

HALF AND HALF

Built 1999 **Engine** Harley-Davidson Shovelhead **Special feature** Inverse paint job: black and orange left side, orange and black right side (pictured below) was based on a sculpture of a 1932 Bugatti Roadster that Ness has in his house.

Like an elegant lady discreetly showing a tantalizing glimpse of thigh, Smooth-Ness allows us to view its beautifully detailed engine. Its superbly sweeping art deco curves were hand-beaten from aluminum by Craig Naff, whose workmanship was so perfect that Arlen Ness actually rode the bike unpainted to several rallies.

The Arlen Ness story continues to this day, with the popularity of custom motorcycles at an all-time high thanks to TV programs like Biker Build-Off. In fact the Top Banana bike pictured on the left, with the man himself aboard, was built to compete in an episode of the program originally televised in 2004.

Ness's son Cory is also now involved with the family business and is a respected custom bike builder in his own right. The two are also involved as design consultants for the Victory Motorcycles company (whose bikes appear on the following pages). Even in his 60s, Arlen Ness is still involved in what he loves most—custom motorcycles.

SMOOTH-NESS

Built 1995 **Engine** Stock Harley-Davidson V2 Evolution 80 cu in (1340cc) **Bodywork** Hand formed aluminum body and trim by Craig Naff

Based on a sculpture of a 1932 Bugatti roadster, Smooth-Ness is a stunningly beautiful evocation of the art deco style that has featured in several Ness bikes

→ with serious attitude—the kind of machine that was born to be a star in a rock band's promo video.

VICTORY MOTORCYCLES

Victory caused a big stir with its initial model, the V92C, in 1997. It was the first all-new American motorcycle for years and won Cycle World's 'Cruiser of the Year' award. The V92C has since been deleted from the model line-up, but the company continues to make a range of quality cruisers.

VICTORY KINGPIN

The Kingpin was released in 2004, initially with the company's 'Freedom' engine of 92 cubic inch (1507cc) capacity and five-speed transmission. For the 2006 model year, these were upgraded to the 100 cubic inch (1634cc) engine and six-speed transmission. It's a classic American cruiser with modern engineering; the Freedom engine is an overhead camshaft design fed by fuel injection, making most Harley-Davidson power units look like dinosaurs by comparison.

The Kingpin Tour (pictured below) adds a clear windshield and a set of saddlebags to the basic model's specification, making it into a practical touring cruiser. The bike's total luggage capacity is actually in excess of 22 gallons (83 liters), including a trunk that can accommodate 20lb (9kg) of biker →

VICTORY KINGPIN

SPECIFICATIONS

Introduced
2004
Engine
Liquid-cooled
50° V-twin
four-stroke
Capacity
100 cu in (1634cc)
Power
N/A
Top speed
N/A

The Victory Kingpin (left) is the American company's flagship cruiser. The Kingpin Tour (below) adds a windshield and saddlebags for extra long–distance capability

VICTORY HAMMER

SPECIFICATIONS

Introduced
2005
Engine
Liquid-cooled
50° V-twin
four-stroke
Capacity
100 cu in (1634cc)
Power
N/A
Top speed
N/A

VICTORY VEGAS JACKPOT

SPECIFICATIONS

Introduced
2006
Engine
Liquid-cooled
50° V-twin
four-stroke
Capacity
100 cu in (1634cc)
Power
N/A
Top speed
N/A

→ belongings. Its long-distance abilities are also helped by a luxury touring seat, rubber-mounted handlebars and vibration-isolating floorboards for both rider and pillion.

VICTORY HAMMER

The Hammer is based on the Vegas, which has been described as 'the bike that saved Victory', with numerous magazine awards transforming the company from a barely-acknowledged also-ran to a major player in a matter of months.

The Vegas incorporated styling guidelines from Arlen and Cory Ness (see Arlen Ness section earlier in this chapter) with a totally new chassis design. The Freedom engine carried forward from the TC, but the rest of the bike incorporated new features not seen on previous Victories.

The most notable of these were: a new rear suspension linkage allowing a 26.5-inch (673mm) seat height, totally new bodywork, a removable passenger seat that does not touch the rear fender, a locking gas cap, warning lights set in the top triple clamp, rubber-mounted handlebars and a revised shifting mechanism.

The Vegas debuted with the 92 cubic inch engine and five-speed transmission, but was upgraded to the 100ci engine and six-speed transmission for the 2006 model year.

The Hammer adds a 10-inch (250mm) section rear tire custom-developed for Victory by Dunlop, giving the bike a distinctive custom look, along with twin Brembo disk brakes up front.

VICTORY VEGAS JACKPOT

The Jackpot was launched in 2006, as the 'extreme custom' of the Victory line-up. It also features the →

The Hammer (right) and the Jackpot (far right) are both based on Victory's Vegas model. Both feature fat 250mm rear tires, but the Jackpot has custom-style paint jobs

The T-Bob has many unique features, but the most remarkable is the rear sprocket (left), which doubles as a brake disc with the caliper biting onto it around the chain

Ducati
T-BOB

Not an official Ducati machine, but a one-off special, this low-rider takes a new approach to the art of customizing

Englishman Roger Allmond was the guy who spent 12 hours a day, seven days a week for 10 months designing and building this unique Ducati-powered 'T-Bob' special. 'T-Bob' stands for 'Techno-Bobber', reflecting the bike's mix of high-tech parts and classic 'bobber' styling.

He put it together with a little help from his friends at Ducati UK, but everything apart from the engine and radiator has been either built from raw materials by Roger or massively modified by him to blend in with the overall concept.

The guys from Ducati did him a deal on a 996cc engine from a crashed test bike and also donated the forks. The frame, a curvaceous interpretation of Ducati's traditional trellis style, was build from scratch with steel tubes, while the gas tank was hand-formed from sheet steel.

The single-sided swingarm was fabricated from aircraft-grade aluminum and every other aluminum component was machined from a solid block or hand-beaten from a sheet of that metal—right down to the levers on the handlebars and even the clutch and brake master cylinders!

Everything is designed to give the bike a beautifully clean look, uncluttered with cables or pipework—even the throttle cable and its mechanism are hidden within the stainless steel handlebars. The wheels are one-offs, too; Roger bought solid-centred blanks from an American specialist and machined spokes into them himself.

The rear tire is huge, with a 300mm (11.8-inch) cross-section, while the rear sprocket is a unique feature, as it also acts as the rear brake disc, with a heavily-modified Brembo caliper biting onto it 'around' the chain.

Roger Allmond's Ducati T-Bob special is a glorious creation. And the great thing is, it's not just a show bike—he really likes to ride it, too.

DUCATI T-BOB

SPECIFICATIONS

Built
2006
Engine
Liquid-cooled
90° V-twin
four-stroke
Capacity
996cc
Power
106bhp
Contact
+44 7785 734923

100 cubic inch Freedom 50° V-twin engine with a six-speed transmission, along with that 250 mm rear Dunlop. In addition to these features, it also has a color-matched frame with a super-low 25.7-inch seat height and extensive custom styling with bold paint schemes. Victory describes it as 'a straight-up custom cruiser with the reliability and quality of a factory-production bike'.

NON-AMERICAN CRUISERS

The USA represents a huge market for motorcycle manufacturers, so naturally home-grown cruisers don't have it all their own way. A British invasion saw the likes of Triumph and BSA taking sales away from Harley-Davidson from the 1960s to the '70s, resulting in the custom cruiser-styled Triumph X75 Hurricane and high-barred versions of the BSA Rocket 3 with detuned engines specifically aimed at the American market.

As the British motorcycle industry waned and finally died, the Japanese factories cashed in, giving their own machines modifications to suit the American market. Italian company Moto Guzzi and German manufacturer BMW have also sold their own takes on the cruiser in America, and with the re-emergence of Triumph it is also now back in the US market once more.

Each of these manufacturers has added their own unique angle to the cruiser formula, giving a greater variety of choice than ever before. Today's American motorcyclist doesn't have to be limited to a V-twin engine; he can choose from V-twins, flat twins, parallel twins or even a triple in the case of Triumph's monstrous Rocket III (see page 62). There's even a choice of a couple of home-grown V8s as power units for the outrageous Boss Hoss (see page 60).

So the American biker is spoilt for choice these days. In the rest of this section the stand-out cruisers produced by the rest of the world have been selected for your perusal. Of course, these models are not just sold in America. The cult of the →

BMW R1200C

SPECIFICATIONS

Introduced
1997
Engine
Oil/air-cooled
flat-twin
four-stroke
Capacity
1170cc
Power
61bhp
Top speed
100mph

→ cruiser has spread from the USA to many other countries in the world where bikers have learned to kick back, relax and just cruise...

BMW R1200C

BMW launched its own particular version of the cruiser in 1997. The R1200C was like no cruiser ever seen before, completely flouting convention. The sophisticated, high-tech machine owed little to anything that had preceded it, with the German company making no attempt to dress it up with pseudo-American design or styling.

The R1200C was unmistakably BMW and it showed in every line and component. Within two years of its launch, the bike had been voted 'Motorcycle of the Year' or 'Cruiser of the Year' in many countries around the world.

The ultimate accolade came when the makers of the James Bond movie series, renowned for their love of high-tech, modern products and innovative design, selected the bike for 007 to ride in the film, Tomorrow Never Dies. The cruiser had moved on a long way from the home-baked choppers of Easy Rider and into the era of technology.

BMW broke the cruiser mould and then stamped all over it when they introduced the 1200C, the most futuristic-looking example of this type of bike ever seen

The bike was powered by a specially tuned and chrome-finished 1170cc version of BMW's signature flat-twin 'boxer' engine delivering 61bhp via a five-speed gearbox and shaft drive to the rear wheel. Its unstressed, low-revving nature proved ideal for relaxed cruising

TRIUMPH AMERICA

In complete contrast to the BMW R1200C's high-tech look, Triumph's America is a very traditional-looking machine, giving the impression that it was the result of a romantic rendez-vous between a Harley-Davidson Sportster and a new-age Triumph Bonneville. Indeed, this bike is often referred to as the 'Bonneville America', even though the only major component it shares with its stablemate is its 865cc parallel-twin engine—and even that is detuned to produce 54bhp rather than the Bonneville's 66bhp.

The America's frame is a basic double-cradle affair fitted with twin shock absorbers in similar style to the Bonneville's, but is 6.4 inches longer and the seat height is 2.2 inches lower. The front end is kicked out more too, to give a classic cruiser's long wheelbase. A hybrid of classic Brit bike and ➔

TRIUMPH AMERICA

SPECIFICATIONS

Introduced
2002
Engine
Parallel twin-cylinder four-stroke
Capacity
865cc
Power
54bhp
Top speed
N/A

A blend of traditional British bike style with the attitude of an American cruiser, the Triumph America aims to rekindle an old transatlantic love affair

KAWASAKI VN2000

SPECIFICATIONS

Introduced
2004
Engine
Liquid-cooled
52° V-twin
four-stroke
Capacity
2053cc (125 cu in)
Power
103bhp
Top speed
124mph

The VN2000 has the biggest production

V-twin ever built to power a motorcycle

→ American cruiser styles, it aims to rekindle the old love affair between US bikers and Triumph.

KAWASAKI VN2000

The VN2000 (called the VN2000 Vulcan in America) is a serial record breaker. For starters, it is the largest capacity motorcycle that Kawasaki has ever produced, with a displacement of 2053cc. Secondly, it was the first production motorcycle engine to break the two-liter barrier, and remains the largest production V-twin built to power a bike.

That's an impressive set of statistics before you even start to consider this motorcycle's sheer physical presence and bulk. We're talking an 820lb (372kg) two-wheeler here, that's the kind of weight that needs a serious amount of muscle just to get the thing off its side stand!

The monster liquid-cooled engine is a clever mix of classic V-twin looks and modern technology. You get push rod valve actuation, which means chromed pushrod tubes visible on the side of the cylinder barrels for that authentic cruiser look, while inside there are forged pistons and hydraulic valve lash adjusters, and the go-juice is fed into the cylinders with electronic fuel injection.

The VN2000's striking visual appearance starts right at the front end, with a huge and unique multi-projector headlamp. Take a step back to appreciate the full 68-inch length of the wheelbase and the lowest seat height in its class at 26.8 inches and you

realise that this is a machine aimed at bikers who like to push through a crowd of onlookers every time they mount their steed.

YAMAHA XV1900 MIDNIGHT STAR

Pay attention, as the name of this big cruiser can be confusing, especially for those who regularly indulge in transatlantic travel. In Europe, this handsome cruiser with styling that leans towards art deco is called the Yamaha XV1900 Midnight Star. However, in the United States Yamaha decided that, as of 2005, it was going to group its whole cruiser range under its 'Star' brand. In America, therefore, this motorcycle is known as the Star Roadliner Midnight.

Now we've got that straight, let's have a look at what makes it tick. The motor in question is a big old lump, but at 1854cc (113 cubic inches) not as outrageously large as that in the Kawasaki on the opposite page. It does, however, have bags of low-down grunt and a pair of ceramic-coated pistons to help it along to its quoted power output of 91bhp.

The high-tech innards tucked away from prying eyes also include Yamaha's EXUP exhaust valve, familiar to owners of sports bikes built by the Japanese company. This is a clever little device which helps to boost mid-range pulling power, so as this cruiser is a relative lightweight considering its engine capacity at 344kg (758lb), this all adds up to produce pretty sprightly performance.

OK, you won't get the 'mine's bigger than ➔

YAMAHA MIDNIGHT STAR

SPECIFICATIONS

Introduced
2005
Engine
Air-cooled
48° V-twin
four-stroke
Capacity
1854cc (113 cu in)
Power
91bhp
Top speed
N/A

The Midnight Star's engine can't quite match the VN2000's for sheer size, but it has bags of grunt

HONDA RUNE

Introduced
2004
Engine
Liquid-cooled
flat-six
four-stroke
Capacity
1832cc (111 cu in)
Power
118bhp
Top speed
123mph

→ yours' bragging rights when standing toe-to-toe with a VN2000 owner, but you can be safe in the knowledge that your bike will not be disgraced if you challenge him to a cruise-off against the clock!

HONDA RUNE

More than any other production motorcycle in this section, the Rune is guaranteed to stop people dead in their tracks with its looks alone. And that's all the more amazing when you consider that it's a product from Honda, a company not renowned for its outrageous styling, even by the normally conservative standards of the Japanese factories.

A development of the Valkyrie, Honda's flat-six-powered mega-cruiser, three different mock-ups of the bike were shown to gauge public opinion in America, and with Honda's US arm pushing for the project to go ahead, the Rune was finally given the green light and made it to production in 2004.

To say this motorcycle is 'styled' would be an understatement. This is hyper-styling, with the Rune's behemoth proportions and the incredible attention to detail producing an effect that is simply breath-taking. Although the bike was built on a production line in Marysville, Ohio, the process was slowed down to such a degree that the result is a virtually hand-built effect, with each machine subjected to an even more fastidious level of quality control than Honda's usual exemplary standard.

The bike's raw statistics are as follows: weight

The massive Honda Rune can stop traffic merely on its looks alone. It is also literally big enough to be used as a roadblock across a single carriageway

fully fuelled 888lb (402kg), making it 10lb (4.5kg) heavier than Honda's Gold Wing mega-tourer; engine 1832cc horizontally-opposed six-cylinder as seen in the Valkyrie and Gold Wing, producing 118bhp via shaft drive; price $27,699 (£14,800).

The cool front-end suspension set-up uses twin pushrods to transfer load through a linkage system, and was very expensive for Honda to make, while the rear uses the adjustable Unit Pro-link setup borrowed from Honda's race bikes, hidden by the Rune's wraparound rear fender.

But the Rune is so much more than just the sum of its parts. It's one of those rare machines with such a cohesion of design it looks as if it has grown organically. Certainly it is one of the most striking production bikes ever. No wonder its owners include the likes of Hollywood star Tom Cruise.

SUZUKI INTRUDER M1800R

The Intruder M1800R (called the Boulevard M109R in the United States) may seem on first glance to have a disadvantage in the battle between the power cruisers to dominate the American market.

At 1783cc, its all-new engine is not the largest in its class, being beaten on capacity by both Yamaha's Midnight Star and Kawasaki's VN2000, but Suzuki claims it is the most powerful V-twin cruiser motor in the world, with its 127bhp bettering both its above rivals. The smooth delivery of all this power is aided by a sophisticated fuel injection system →

SUZUKI INTRUDER M1800R

SPECIFICATIONS

Introduced
2006
Engine
LIquid-cooled
54° V-twin
four-stroke
Capacity
1783cc
Power
127bhp
Top speed
138mph

Suzuki claims the Intruder's 1783cc engine is the most powerful V–twin engine in the world, putting out an impressive 127bhp

BOSS HOSS

Introduced
1990
Engine
Liquid-cooled V8
four-stroke
Capacity
350 cu in (5700cc) or
502 cu in (8200cc)
Power
355bhp or 502bhp
Top speed
150mph-plus

derived from Suzuki's sports bikes and controlled by a powerful 32-bit processor. Its 315kg (694lb) dry weight means it is relatively light for a monster cruiser, and aims to disprove the idea that 'biggest is best', a philosophy that the makers of the cruiser pictured below has taken to the max...

BOSS HOSS

If you find the Honda Rune a little understated, the VN2000 a bit gutless and the Triumph Rocket III somewhat under-endowed in the engine department,

what you probably need is a Boss Hoss. Take a good look at the photographs on these two pages and check out the engines in these bikes. No , your eyes are not deceiving you, these really are motorcycles powered by big, bad, all-American Chevrolet V8s!

Boss Hoss has been producing these two-wheeled leviathans for 15 years, fine-tuning the mating of the iconic automobile engine with the two-wheeled chassis as it went.

This results in the two current Boss Hoss models pictured here (although trikes are also →

The Boss Hoss is living proof of the American saying 'there's no replacement for displacement' offering a choice of two huge Chevrolet V8s, making them motorcycles that are simply unsurpassed for sheer size and power

SPECIFICATIONS

Introduced
2004
Engine
Liquid-cooled
three-cylinder
four-stroke
Capacity
2294cc (140 cu in)
Power
140bhp
Top speed
136mph

Triumph
ROCKET III

Big, bold and British,
the Rocket III cruiser
packs the performance
of a serious sports bike

Triumph's mega-cruiser has the biggest
production motorcycle engine in the world,
a 2294cc (140 cu in) triple putting out 140bhp

Boss Hoss motorcycles may hold the record for the largest capacity engine in a two-wheeler, but the power plant in Triumph's awesome Rocket III is certainly the biggest in large-scale production. A 2.3-liter (140 cubic inch) three-cylinder monster motor, it pumps out 140bhp, which also makes it the most powerful cruiser engine in series production.

The result of all this power, as well as truckloads of low-down grunt, is acceleration that can keep the Rocket ahead of some serious sports bike competition—for a while, at least.

When it was launched, Triumph claimed that it was quicker than Suzuki's hyperbike, the Hayabusa, at the time the fastest accelerating production bike on the planet. Independent magazine tests proved that the big Triumph was, indeed quicker than the Hayabusa from 0-40mph, an incredible feat for a 320kg (705lb) cruiser.

The rest of the Rocket III matches up to the massive motor, which is not arranged across the frame as with Triumph's other triples but turned through 90° so that its crankshaft is in line with the wheels. You have to see one of these bikes 'in the metal' to fully appreciate the scale of it. The gas tank, seat and exhaust pipes are all supersize items, giving riders the sort of 'king of the road' feeling that SUV drivers enjoy in the automobile world.

Despite its size and weight, however, the Rocket III is not an intimidating machine for those who are used to powerful motorcycles. The low 740mm (29-inch) seat height helps to avoid any teetering moments at stop lights and the fact that most of the weight is carried as near to the road as possible makes this big beast surprisingly manageable and manoeuvrable.

Once you get the hang of the size of the thing, the Rocket III is a pussycat to pootle around town. The power is smooth and gradual if you're gentle with the throttle, but if you give it a big handful the

bike seems to go into warp drive. It's a seriously arm-stretching experience and that big engine just keeps on pulling like a steam train in every gear.

With a fat 240mm-section rear tire, you would not expect this bike to handle well, but it acquits itself pretty well in that area compared to some other big cruisers. Suspension is conventional, with 43mm upside-down forks up front and twin shock absorbers at the rear.

Riders who do a lot of two-up riding tend to replace these rear shocks with uprated items to stop the rear end wallowing too much, as well as fitting an aftermarket gel seat for extra comfort and to avoid getting earache from the passenger.

Overall, Triumph's Rocket III is an impressive machine, a big British bike that is trying hard to capture the hearts and minds of American riders.

The Boss Hoss's 502 cubic-inch (8.2-litre) big block Chevy V8 engine pumps out a momentous 502bhp

→ available). You get an option of the 'small block' Chevy V8 with a capacity of 350 cubic inches (5.7 litres) which develops 355bhp in basic form, or the 'big block' with 502 cubic inches (8.2 litres) giving an arm-wrenching 502bhp.

All this power is transmitted through a two-speed automatic transmission with reverse gear; you really need the latter because the 'small block' bike weighs 1100lb (500kg) and the 'big block' tips the scales at 1300lb (590kg). That's not the kind of mass that's easy to paddle backwards when you're sitting astride it!

As if that's not enough pure American excess, your Boss Hoss can also be hopped up with a factory-fitted turbocharger and nitrous oxide injection, bringing the big V8's output up to near an astonishing 1,000bhp!

The list of factory options also includes more practical and cosmetic add-ons to personalise these massive motorcycles, such as highway pegs, backrests, handlebar risers, a fairing with built-in audio system, a quick-release windshield and a sissy-bar/luggage rack/hard luggage combo.

Boss Hoss is living proof that everything is bigger in America. Its massive motorcycles make the current cruiser engine capacity war look like a battle between a bunch of minimotos.

TOURING MOTORCYCLES

BMW K1200LT

TOURING *Motorcycles*

Hitting the highway on a big trip is an exhilarating sensation. Leaving behind all your cares to experience new landscapes on a motorcycle is one of the greatest feelings in the world. You can do it on any bike, but these ultimate tourers have the ability to make a long journey as comfortable as sitting in your favourite armchair and to turn it into the trip of a lifetime

It is perfectly possible to go touring on any motorcycle ever made. Hardy souls with adventurous spirits have undertaken epic trips on machines as lowly as Honda's C50 Cub moped, and will continue to do so in cases where wanderlust outweighs the tourists's ability or desire to pay large sums of money for the latest state-of-the-art touring motorcycles.

While this spirit of adventure is to be applauded, we are dealing in this book with ultimate motorcycles. And there are today a select band of highly specialised touring machines that come equipped with every creature comfort imaginable in order to make covering vast mileages as pleasurable an experience as possible.

With specifications that would, until fairly recently, only have been found on top-flight motor cars, these motorcycles pander to the long-distance rider's every need—and the needs of the pillion passenger sitting behind, too. Their large-capacity engines can devour intercontinental mileages with ease and their dimensions are designed to make the trip as comfortable as possible.

In short, if your finances can handle it, these are the machines of choice if you're planning that classic coast-to-coast tour of the USA or a continental ➔

HARLEY-DAVIDSON ELECTRA GLIDE

SPECIFICATIONS

Introduced
2006
Engine
Air-cooled
45° V-twin
four-stroke
Capacity
103 cu in (1688cc)
Power
80bhp (estimated)
Top speed
N/A

→ grand tour taking in the most spectacular scenery that Europe has to offer. They are the ultimate touring motorcycles available today.

HARLEY-DAVIDSON ELECTRA GLIDE

'Electra Glide' is probably the most evocative model name in the Harley-Davidson line-up, with a history that goes back for decades. And the company's Custom Vehicle Operations department, which was specifically set up to put together the ultimate in exclusive Harleys, has come up with the most fully-loaded Electra Glide ever.

This motorcycle is a huge and imposing luxury tourer with every conceivable aid to making mile-eating trips as comfortable as possible. The major upgrade is in the engine department, with Harley's latest 103 cubic inch (1688cc) Twin Cam, the biggest-ever factory-supplied version of its trademark 45° V-twin. This impressive power plant hauls 885lb (388kg) of motorcycle along the highway.

The leather-covered 'Tour-Pak' comprises a 'trunk' unit with integrated pillion backrest and chrome luggage rack, with LEDs to light up the interior of the trunk. Dual heated seats combine with heated grips to make winter touring bearable, while the top-quality Harman/Kardon sound system designed specifically for the bike includes an AM/FM/CB/Intercom plus a CD/MP3 player and 40-watt-

You want fully loaded? You got it! Harley-Davidson's Electra Glide has got the lot, right down to the cigar lighter!

per-channel amplifier with front and rear speakers.

There is even a built-in garage door opener and receiver that you can program to operate when you flick the headlight high-beam switch in front of your garage door, a cigar lighter and another power outlet to make it easy to plug in electrical gizmos.

The Harley-Davidson Screamin' Eagle Ultra Classic Electra Glide is not only a motorcycle with one of the longest names around, it is also $19,795 (£22,995 in the UK) of pure American luxury.

MOTO GUZZI CALIFORNIA

The Moto Guzzi California may not boast all the creature comforts and electronic gizmos that the other three bikes in this section are laden with, but it does have the kind of timeless style that makes grown men go all misty-eyed and banish rational thought from their minds.

Buying a Moto Guzzi is never a logical decision and if you consider the raw facts, the latest version of the California, the 'Vintage' model launched in 2006 is outgunned by the other three tourers here in all respects. But we're talking about a living classic here, a model that has been around since the very early '70s, the coolest bike the California Highway Patrol ever went to work on.

The California Vintage is powered by that classic Guzzi hallmark, the 90° V-twin engine mounted →

MOTO GUZZI CALIFORNIA VINTAGE

SPECIFICATIONS

Introduced
2006
Engine
Air-cooled
90° V-twin
four-stroke
Capacity
1064cc (65 cu in)
Power
73bhp
Top speed
N/A

The Moto Guzzi California has been around for 35 years, and the 2006 'Vintage' pictured here harks back to the original model's timeless sense of style

HONDA GOLD WING

SPECIFICATIONS

Introduced
2006
Engine
Flat
six-cylinder
four-stroke
Capacity
1823cc
Power
118bhp
Top speed
130mph

→ across the frame with the cylinders hanging out there in the breeze on either side. These days it has a 1064cc capacity, much bigger than the original 750, and produces a very relaxed 73bhp.

But hey, it's the looks and the style that are the turn-on with this bike: the stark black and white colorscheme, the spoked wheels, the chrome that coats the exhaust pipes, front fender and luggage rack, the foglamps, and the crash bars which protect the engine and fixed panniers. Go touring on a Guzzi California and you always arrive in style.

HONDA GOLD WING

The latest incarnation of Honda's Gold Wing super-tourer is powered by a 1823cc flat-six engine giving a super-smooth 118bhp of power to haul this 363kg (800lb) behemoth along. Progress in both directions is as effortless as possible, with cruise control and even a thumb-operated slow-speed reverse gear.

This machine takes high-tech touring to new heights, with a bewildering array of gadgets and luxury appointments, at a cost of £17,399 in the UK ($22,799 in the USA). There's an anti-lock braking system, computer-controlled rear suspension with two memory settings to ensure pillion comfort at all times, plus a satellite navigation system with color screen to ensure you never get lost on the highway.

Naturally, there's also a premium audio system featuring an 80-watt per channel amplifier powering six speakers, while the remote-locking luggage trunk

The Gold Wing is loaded with every conceivable luxury and creature comfort. Soon you will even be able to specify an airbag!

can house an optional CD changer if required.

As this book went to press, Honda was also on the verge of offering a feature for the Gold Wing that is a first in motorcycling—a fully integrated rider airbag!

BMW K1200 LT

The BMW K1200 LT is a super-tourer with a superbly cohesive design. BMW calls it an 'all-inclusive motorcycle body', with the fairing, fuel tank, seats, luggage and even the exhaust system blended into a single unit instead of being individual components all grouped around an engine and frame.

This triumph of form and function is powered by BMW's relentlessly reliable 1171cc 16-valve, liquid-cooled, in-line four-cylinder engine producing 116bhp.

Its job is to haul 378.5kg (835lb) of bike around.

Standard equipment on the K1200 LT includes BMW's Integral ABS, with the anti-lock system backing up the linked brakes which apply braking across both wheels when either the hand or foot brake are actuated, for safer riding.

BMW's unique suspension ensures plush ride quality, while a windshield with continuous electrical adjustment and additional wind guide vanes provides excellent weather protection. The £15,215 ($22,195 in the USA) K1200 LT Lux version features heated seats and grips, cruise control, a CD multi-changer, a high windshield, and a topcase luggage rack with high-level brake light. It's a package that can easily take even the most arduous trip in its stride.

SPECIFICATIONS

Introduced
2004
Engine
In-line
four-cylinder
four-stroke
Capacity
1171cc
Power
116bhp
Top speed
130mph

With its 'all-inclusive motorcycle body', all the component parts of the K1200 LT work together for maximum touring potential

BMW K1200S

SPORTS *Motorcycles*

Focused on speed, lightness and nimble handling, most sports bikes are designed to give the rider a taste of the track sensations experienced by racers. In recent years, the race for performance has been hastened by the competition between Japanese factories to produce the top superbike. But there are some exceptions which take their own course...

Ever since the early days of powered two-wheelers, the racing instinct has been a force that has propelled the development of motorcycles to ever greater heights of performance.

The tuning of production street machines to meet the demands of the track is a device that has been used by manufacturers since time immemorial. The motivation for this, along with the pure glory of producing a race-winning machine, was the hope that success on the track would raise the profile of a bike and its maker.

By beating the opposition on the most famous and demanding circuits in the world and in the most prestigious racing championships, manufacturers aimed to drum up sales of road bikes to the general public on the back of that success.

For many decades, however, sampling the delights of these track-focused machines was the preserve of motorcycle racers and the privileged few who could afford the premium of buying high-specification bikes. The biker in the street could only dream of the acceleration, speed and handling experienced by the guys who competed in world-famous races such as the UK's Isle of Man TT or on high-speed banked tracks like Daytona in the USA.

Producing motorcycles that would replicate ➔

With its combination of lightweight
aluminum frame, 100bhp 749cc engine and
race bike looks, the original GSX-R750 of
1985 was a truly revolutionary sports bike

→ the looks and performance of these racing thoroughbreds and putting them on sale to enthusiasts as limited edition specials had been tried, but the market for such bikes was small.

It wasn't until the 1980s that a mass-produced bike with race track performance and styling was offered to the general public. The company that made that quantum leap was Suzuki, which established the modern concept of the 'race replica' when it released the GSX-R750.

Here was a motorcycle that echoed the looks of the bikes campaigned by top-class racers on the world's most famous circuits, but in street-legal form. Improvements in mass-production techniques allowed the bike to be built in numbers previously unheard of. The era of the high-performance sports bike for the masses had begun…

SUZUKI GSX-R750

Based on the successful GSR1000R XR41 works race bike, the GSX-R750 stunned the motorcycling world with its light weight and high performance when it burst onto the scene in 1985. The Suzuki engineers in charge of its creation dubbed the project 'Born on the circuit, back to the circuit', a phrase which encapsulates the bike's race-bred ethos perfectly.

With components that had been race-developed for lightness and efficiency, the GSX-R was leaner and meaner than any previous road bike. It had the looks of a machine that had just been lifted straight off the grid of an endurance race and deposited in your local Suzuki dealership. And anyone who had a bike licence could walk in off the street, pay the man behind the counter and tear off to their favourite stretch of highway to scare themselves silly trying to emulate their heroes' exploits on the race track.

The GSX-R used the in-line four-cylinder engine layout that had become the proven provider of smooth, high-revving power for Suzuki's road and race bikes. Air and oil cooled, the 749cc motor produced 100bhp at the crankshaft, giving a potential top speed of 145mph. Its chassis featured the first aluminum frame on a production road bike and was incredibly light, the whole bike weighing only 178kg dry. A full race fairing with twin headlights reflected the GSX-R's racing heritage.

The original GSX-R750 was a huge sales success for Suzuki, becoming the tool of choice for thrill-seeking bikers the world over. And not only did it succeed at giving blue-collar guys a buzz from riding round their local lanes, the bike also became a successful race machine in its own right. It formed the basis for the Suzuki Cup, which transformed the face of motorcycle racing and gave rise to a new class of professional and semi-pro racers worldwide, also gaining great success in world-class superbike and endurance competition.

Because of its historical significance, original examples of the GSX-R750 in good condition are now highly prized by collectors keen to own the first true race replica of the modern era – a bike which raised the bar for street-legal sports bikes and inspired a whole generation of imitators…

THE RACE FOR PERFORMANCE

Suzuki had set a new benchmark with its GSX-R750, bolstering its image and its sales figures in the process. So it was only natural that its rival manufacturers would try to muscle in on the action. This heralded an ongoing performance war which continues to this day, spawning developments in motorcycle technology and components that have led to the dizzying heights of acceleration, speed and agility of today's street-legal sports bikes.

The Japanese motorcycle industry, already well established as the world leader when the GSX-R first emerged, has largely proved the motive force behind this continual upgrading and improvement. Since the Suzuki created the production race replica formula, a continual parade of machines has emerged from Japan, gradually becoming lighter, more powerful and with ever-increasing abilities in terms of suspension, braking and agility. However, only →

SUZUKI GSX-R750

SPECIFICATIONS

Introduced
1985
Engine
In-line four-cylinder four-stroke
Capacity
749cc
Power
100bhp
Top speed
145mph

" **Suzuki established the concept of the race replica with the GSX-R750** "

"The FireBlade pushed the quest for performance to the next level"

→ a select few of the models produced by these factories is worthy to stand alongside the Suzuki as an 'ultimate' motorcycle by taking a similar step towards performance bike nirvana.

HONDA CBR900RR FIREBLADE

On the face of it, the basic formula of the FireBlade (known as the CBR900RR in the USA) doesn't vary wildly from that of the GSX-R750 or its larger brother, the GSX-R1100. Powered by a four-cylinder, four-stroke engine aligned across the frame and clothed in race-inspired bodywork, it simply looks like a development of the original race replica format. But the original FireBlade was not a race bike adapted for the road, it was a purpose-designed road bike—and one which pushed the quest for performance to the next level.

As is often the case with innovations which effect a revolutionary change on any form of industry, the FireBlade was the brainchild of one man. A young Honda engineer by the name of Tadao Baba was the guy who dreamed up the idea. He felt he could create something so much better than the high-capacity sports bikes of the day, which were heavy, cumbersome machines. Honda's management gave him the funding to develop his concept of a street →

HONDA CBR900RR FIREBLADE

SPECIFICATIONS

Introduced
1992
Engine
In-line four-cylinder four-stroke
Capacity
893cc
Power
124bhp
Top speed
164mph

With its 124bhp, 893cc engine and compact chassis, the CBR900RR proved a potent package of performance and agility

YAMAHA YZF-R1

SPECIFICATIONS

Introduced
1998
Engine
In-line
four-cylinder
four-stroke
Capacity
998cc
Power
160bhp
Top speed
170mph

The R1 caused a sensation with its aggressive looks and simply astounding performance

→ bike with a high-output engine in the lightweight and compact chassis of one of the company's 600cc bikes, and the result was one of the most ground-breaking motorcycles of modern times.

The FireBlade emerged in 1992, packing the performance of an 893cc engine with the agility of a 600cc machine—and all combined in an easy-to-ride package that meant you didn't have to be a hairy-chested he-man or a wannabe racer to enjoy it. OK, it was beaten on capacity by the 1000cc competition, but it produced 124bhp and its dry weight of 185kg combined with its compact, agile chassis took road bike performance and handling into another league, backed up with a 164mph top speed.

It was exactly what the motorcycle buying public wanted. The new Honda's excellent power-to-weight ratio, plus its massively improved dynamics, rider-friendly nature, fine build quality and reliability made it a big success. It's a mass-produced motorcycle whose name continues to grace Honda's flagship superbike to this day, and although its popularity means it doesn't have the exclusivity of more exotic

machines Tadao Baba's FireBlade stands out as a bike that brought about a momentous change in the world of sports motorcycles.

The FireBlade enjoyed its reign as the world's top production sports motorcycle until 1998, when Yamaha raised the bar with its incredible R1.

YAMAHA YZF-R1

Yamaha's aim in developing the YZF-R1 was simple: to produce the lightest, fastest, best-handling production sports motorcycle on the planet. As Honda made gradual improvements to the FireBlade, slowly increasing its engine capacity and power, Yamaha engineers beavered away at producing a bike that would outperform it in every way.

When it appeared in 1998, the R1's aggressive styling signalled its intent and had sports bike fans reaching for their cheque books due to its looks alone. But it was the technological breakthroughs, and the way they combined in one machine to make it such an exhilarating ride, which propelled the R1 to the top of the performance and sales charts.

Yamaha had completely redesigned its Genesis engine for the R1, producing a shorter, lighter 998cc unit that used five valves per cylinder to help it kick out 160bhp. Just as important as that impressive power figure was the amount of low-down grunt the engine produced, giving an incredibly flexible power delivery. It was possible to accelerate cleanly from 20mph to its top speed of 170mph in top gear! Mid-range response was aided by Yamaha's electronic 'EXUP' exhaust valve system.

Given its head as it screamed towards the 10,000rpm where peak power was produced, the bike had such blistering acceleration that some white-faced R1 buyers were known to have traded their bikes back in very quickly after being plain terrified of the bike's pure speed.

Less easily intimidated sports bike fans revelled in the R1's performance, however. Along with its awesome power, the Yamaha also had sharper, more precise handling than any other street-legal machine

in production. The new, shorter engine allowed for a shorter wheelbase which, when combined with a new lightweight twin-spar aluminum frame using Yamaha's Delta Box technology, gave an unbeatable combination of stability and nimbleness when cornering. At 177kg (389lbs), the R1 was also lighter than most 600cc sports bikes of the day, allowing the rider to flick it through a series of bends with a level of control that bordered on the telepathic.

The Honda FireBlade had essentially been a 'parts bin' motorcycle, assembled from existing components which were adapted to suit the purpose, but the R1 was all new and purpose-designed from the ground up. The cohesive design included top-quality suspension and brake parts, completing a package that made every other two-wheeler on the road look like a clumsy dinosaur. →

The R1 was the lightest, fastest, best handling street motorcycle on earth in the late '90s. Some owners were so overwhelmed by its warp-speed acceleration that they quickly exchanged their R1s for slower machines!

" **The R1 made every other bike on the road look like a clumsy dinosaur** "

Introduced
2005
Engine
In-line
four-cylinder
four-stroke
Capacity
998cc
Power
175bhp
Top speed
186mph (limited)

Suzuki
GSX-R1000

King of the roads in the superbike class, the GSX-R1000 K6 has also become a world-beating race bike on the track

Whether on a race circuit or on the road, the GSX-R1000 K6 is a winner

*I*ntense competition between the Japanese 'Big Four' manufacturers of Honda, Yamaha, Kawasaki and Suzuki over the past decade has accelerated the development of the superbike to ever more dizzying heights. At the time of writing, the current top dog is Suzuki's latest version of its long-running GSX-R1000, the K6, launched in 2005.

Taking the Japanese passion for miniaturisation to new heights, this is one tiny, incredibly light and awesomely powerful motorcycle. Although its claimed maximum power figure of 175bhp is beaten by the claims of some of its competitors, independent tests by motorcycle publications have proven that, in real terms, the GSX-R is the most powerful production superbike available to the general public today.

Developments in technology gained from race bikes, combined with the use of ever lighter and more sophisticated components, make this Suzuki an unfeasibly compact rocketship.

The in-line four-cylinder engine features internal components pared down to be lightest weight possible, with superbly engineered mechanicals that a few years ago would have only been seen in engines used for MotoGP racing.

Race bike features such as a slipper clutch which stops the rear wheel locking up when downchanging under hard braking, and radially-mounted brake calipers, give the GSX-R1000 the look and feel of a racer. The success of the Suzuki in World Superbike racing, winning the 2005 championship at the hands of Troy Corser, speaks volumes for the bike's sporting abilities.

Seeing a new GSX-R1000 for the first time is a shock, as it is so tiny. Experiencing it accelerating from 0-60mph in just over three seconds and howling on to its top speed (as with all current Japanese superbikes, limited to 186mph thanks to a 'gentlemen's agreement' between the 'Big Four') requires complete re-calibration of the senses.

That such a machine can be bought in the UK for £8799 ($10,849 in the USA) brand new and used legally on public roads is simply astonishing. In terms of bangs per buck, the latest GSX-R1000 has everything else on the street licked.

→ Yamaha had even carried out intensive work on the bike's ergonomics, so that although the R1 was short it wasn't cramped, giving plenty of room for the rider to shift his weight around during high-speed cornering.

The R1 was king of the roads for years to come, a machine which had elevated road bike performance towards the stratospheric realms of Formula One race car acceleration and top speeds that had previously been the preserve of racing motorcycles. Surely this had to be the all-time zenith of sports motorcyles, an achievement that could never be surpassed—no one could make a machine that was lighter, more powerful and with sharper handling than this, could they?

Well they could, they did—and they continue to do so! The spirit of human competition pushes the race for performance ever onwards. The R1's quantum leap forward served to ignite the 1000cc 'litre bike' war between the 'Big Four' Japanese factories which continues to this day, as they produce ever lighter, faster and sharper machines in the quest for superbike sales supremacy. The ultimate current mass-production sports bike is the latest incarnation of Suzuki's GSX-R1000, the K6 (see left). Until someone makes something even lighter, faster and sharper, that is...

MEANWHILE, IN THE REST OF THE WORLD...

As the war raged between the 'Big Four' Japanese manufacturers of Suzuki, Honda, Yamaha and Kawasaki to produce the ultimate performer in the four-cylinder 1000cc superbike market, other manufacturers based elsewhere in the world continued to develop their sports motorcycles in their own particular way.

Despite the massive dominance of the Japanese factories in both racing motorcycles on the track and selling them in the showrooms, companies outside of the Orient have managed to provide customers with products which express different attitudes to the whole sports bike concept. This has given →

With its fizzing two-stroke performance and a fantastic chassis which gives super-sharp handling and allows outrageous angles of lean, the RS250 is a real little superbike slayer

Aprilia followed up its successful RS250 by launching into the superbike market with the RSV1000 Mille. The street bike was a big sales success, while the race version did well in World Superbikes

APRILIA RS250

Introduced
1994
Engine
Liquid cooled
V-twin
two-stroke
Capacity
249cc
Power
60bhp
Top speed
126mph

SPECIFICATIONS

APRILIA RSV MILLE

Introduced
1998
Engine
Liquid cooled
60° V-twin
four-stroke
Capacity
998cc
Power
128bhp
Top speed
169mph

SPECIFICATIONS

→ riders a wider choice of machines and resulted in the production of some exceptional sports bikes.

APRILIA RS250

One company that has grown carved its own distinct niche in the sports bike market is the Italian company Aprilia. It started in the late 1960s building scooters and off-road competition machines, but by the late '80s had begun to score successes on the race track. Concentrating on the smaller capacity classes of 125cc and 250cc in the Grand Prix World Championships, Aprilia continued to develop its race bikes and rack up racing victories.

The time had come for the company to capitalise on the sporting glory of its race bikes by selling a road-legal replica to the public, and in 1995 the RS250 was born. Essentially based on the race bike on which Italian superstar Max Biaggi had won the world 250cc Grand Prix Championship in 1994, it was powered by an engine bought in from Suzuki—the Japanese company's 250cc V-twin two-stroke engine from its own RGV250 race replica. With the

engine slotted into a superb chassis which benefited from the experience gained from making the race bike such a winner, and with bodywork which echoed the racer's style, the package was complete.

The result was one of the purest race replicas ever to become available to the general public. As the race bike dominated the World 250cc Grand Prix class in the late '90s, the road-legal version was a winner with enthusiastic riders due to its berserk two-stroke performance and incredible agility.

The RS250 has to be revved hard to get the best out of its 60bhp V-twin. A typically peaky two-stroke motor, it has a narrow power band near the top of its rev range which means that keeping the engine on the boil combined with rapid gear changes are required for maximum acceleration.

This little Aprilia can punch well above its weight thanks to the combination of that fizzing engine and the incredible corner speed and lean angles allowed by the superb chassis. And boy, does it look the part, too. The full fairing, beautifully shaped and polished aluminum swingarm and distinctive →

" The RS250 is one of the purest race replicas ever available to the general public "

APRILIA RSVR NERA

SPECIFICATIONS

Introduced
2004
Engine
Liquid cooled
V-twin
four-stroke
Capacity
998cc
Power
141bhp
Top speed
174mph

→ graphics all scream RACING with typical Italian style. A redesign in 1998 resulted in an even sleeker, racier look, plus improved performance and suspension.

Ironically, it was the RS250 road bike's affinity to its racing brother that brought about its demise. Then, as now, the 250 Grand Prix class was competed in exclusively by two-stroke machines, which produce 'dirtier' emissions than four-strokes. With the advent of ever-tightening anti-smog legislation,

The ultimate Aprilia RSV was the Nera of 2003 with carbon-fibre body panels and magnesium wheels

the RS250 was forced out of production in 2002.

Today, the model is becoming more and more collectable as good examples become rarer. This is definitely one to mark down as a future classic.

SUPERBIKES ITALIAN-STYLE

Encouraged by the continuing success of its racers in the 125 and 250cc Grand Prix Championships and the popularity of its RS250 race replica, Aprilia decided it was ready to mix it with the big boys in the 1000cc superbike class. It set about designing its own high-capacity machine, with the aim of both

racing it in the World Superbike Championship and selling a road-legal version in dealerships.

Aprilia had grown rapidly as a company, reaping the benefits of its policy of out-sourcing. The Italian firm does not make any parts for its motorcycles, relying on third-party suppliers for components, which are assembled at the company's factory. Aprilia struck a deal with Austrian firm Rotax to supply 998cc, 128bhp four-stroke 60° V-twin engines.

Flying in the face of the Japanese superbikes' endless quest for miniaturisation and ever lighter weight, the RSV is a relatively large motorcycle. With a 189kg dry weight, it was markedly heavier than the cutting-edge Japanese bikes, but carried its weight well and is renowned as a fine handling machine.

The bike was christened the RSV Mille (Italian for one thousand) and although it could not match the visual impact of its Italian V-twin superbike rival, the Ducati 996, the Aprilia had no shortage of sex appeal. The buying public certainly took it to their hearts, too, with the Aprilia ending up outselling its more headline-grabbing competitor, which went some way to redressing the fact that it never emulated the dominance of the Ducati in the World Superbike series, despite some success.

It was the combination of keen pricing, reliability and the fact that it had a less complex engine and therefore more affordable servicing costs than the Ducati which made it such a showroom success.

After the standard RSV Mille appeared, a number of upgraded models were introduced, including the Mille R with OZ racing wheels and quality Ohlins suspension as standard and the even more high-spec and track-focused Factory.

The ultimate Mille is the RSVR Nera, a version of the heavily revised model which was introduced in 2004 Based on the Factory, the Nera was fully clothed in high-tech carbon-fibre body panels and featured an exhaust system plus nuts, bolts and fasteners made of superlight titanium.

Also included in the package were a VIP visit to a round of the Grand Prix championship with

hospitality from Aprilia's MotoGP team plus tailor-made Dainese leathers, an Aprilia helmet and a visit to the Aprilia factory. Only 200 Neras were ever produced, their exclusivity reflected in the £25,000 ($47,000) price tag

A NAME FROM THE PAST

The revival of Ducati, largely on the back of the incredible success of its glamorous 916 in the World Superbike Championships, gave hope to other →

BENELLI TORNADO

SPECIFICATIONS

Introduced
2003
Engine
In-line three-cylinder four-stroke
Capacity
898cc
Power
144bhp
Top speed
169mph

The Benelli Tornado differs from other Italian superbikes as it has a three-cylinder engine. The unique twin fans in the tail unit (top) direct cooling air over the underseat radiator

→ Italian marques which were struggling as Ducati had for many years—and even those which had disappeared altogether. Benelli was one such company of the latter type. Probably best known for its Sei ('Six' in Italian) six-cylinder model of the 1980s, the company had disappeared from the map of Italian bike manufacturers in the late '80s.

But it came back fighting in 2003 with the individually-styled and engineered Tornado superbike, emphasising the machine's sports focus and racing intentions by first being revealed at the world-famous Isle of Man TT races the previous year.

With its 898cc in-line across-the-frame three-cylinder engine and sharply angular styling, it was distinctly different to every other superbike on the market. The rear end was given a unique twist by the integration of two fans underneath the tail unit to direct cooling air to the underseat radiator.

Power and weight, at 140bhp and 185kg, made for serious superbike performance, but although the £22,000 ($41,000) price for the original high-spec Tornado was lowered for the base model, this has remained very much a cult bike, which will add to its rarity and desirability in years to come.

AMERICAN SPORTS BIKES

American motorcycle sport has traditionally been dominated by flat track racing, in which competition takes part on mile-long dirt oval tracks. This has produced a peculiarly American breed of sports bikes, epitomised by Harley-Davidson's XR750 (see over the page and Classics section).

Nothing like the road racing machines produced in Japan and Europe, they have a brutal attraction all of their own. But there have been a couple of times in Harley's history when the company attempted to embrace European style and then emulate the success of Ducati on the World Superbike stage.

Willie G Davidson, grandson of one of the founders of Harley-Davidson, was the man behind a model that was a big break with the company's tradition in the form of the XLCR1000 'Café →

Ducati 916

A true icon of motorcycling, this 'two-wheeled Ferrari' combined racing glory with the ultimate in Italian glamour

The Ducati 916 is a superbike superstar. The pure beauty of its sleek muscularity caused a sensation on its launch in 1993, and it was so much more than just a pretty face.

Designed by a team led by motorcycle styling and engineering genius Massimo Tamburini, the 916's form had a very serious purpose. Ducati had pulled itself from the brink of financial collapse on the back of the successes of its 851 and 888 race bikes in the World Superbike Championship, a production bike-based race series which started in 1988. The 916's job was to continue that racing success and reap the rewards by selling enough street-legal versions of the bike in Ducati dealerships to help keep the company afloat.

Powered by a 916cc engine with Ducati's traditional 90° V-twin layout, its cylinders aligned in line with the frame, it also featured the company's trademark 'desmodromic' cylinder head with its system of valves closed by a cam rather than springs. With high-level exhaust pipes that exited directly underneath the seat and a single-sided swingarm, the 916's streamlined shape helped it to win races as well as hearts.

Backing up the 114bhp of throbbing power from the big V-twin, the bike's frame was of traditional Ducati design—a 'trellis' of steel tubes giving exceptional rigidity. This gave the 916 rock-solid cornering stability to compliment the light steering, producing a handling package that made it hard to beat on the track.

Indeed, the Ducati enjoyed as much sporting success as it had sex appeal, with Englishman Carl Fogarty taking the bike to four World Superbike Championships in the 1990s. The company had a winner on its hands, and the shape remained unchanged until 2002, with the engine capacity increasing first to 996cc and then on to 998cc in its final incarnation.

Apart from the original single-seat Strada version, a Biposto twin-seater was also offered. Following that, over the years a series of special editions emerged. They included the Senna, a tribute to Formula One racing legend Ayrton Senna finished in gun metal grey with red wheels, and the Carl Fogarty replica with its white tail unit and mechanical upgrades. Other high-performance derivatives included the SP and SPS. The final model, the 998, was powered by a 998cc 'Testastretta' (narrow head) engine with 123bhp.

The 916 is one of those rare bikes that are instant classics—and remains so to this day.

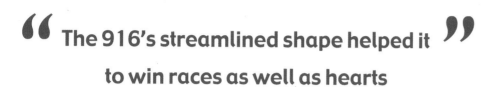

The 916's streamlined shape helped it to win races as well as hearts

DUCATI 916

Introduced
1993
Engine
Liquid cooled
90° V-twin
four-stroke
Capacity
916cc
Power
114bhp
Top speed
158mph

> Racer'. 'Willie G', as he is better known, joined Harley's design department in 1963 and proved a powerful force behind changing the firm's previously staid ideas of motorcycle styling.

HARLEY–DAVIDSON CAFE RACER

Based on the Sportster, the XLCR1000 was styled along the lines of English café racers—the machines raced from café to café by the 'ton-up boys' of the '50s and '60s—with drop handlebars and a simple fairing around the headlight. Aimed at the stoplight racers of America's West Coast, the XLCR featured a lightweight triangulated space frame, with its 61

cubic inch (998cc) 68bhp V-twin pushing along 515lb (234kg) of motorcycle to a possible maximum speed of 110mph. To slow things down, the Café Racer became the first Harley-Davidson to be fitted with triple disc brakes.

The all-black steel tank and fiberglass tail piece coupled with the unique black Siamese exhausts gave the machine a truly sinister look, but it was too radical a departure from accepted Harley style to be a big success, with sales figures of under 3,200 from its 1977-79 production run. But that has only served to make it a sought-after motorcycle; its subsequent rarity and the fact that it bucked the traditional

> "American motorcycle sport has traditionally been domionated by flat track racing, which has produced a peculiar breed of sports bikes"

The brutally beautiful Harley–Davidson XR750 has dominated American dirt-track racing for decades

Harley trend of laid-back cruisers ensure that it is a prized collector's item today,

It is nowhere near as rare as the machine with which Harley-Davidson staged an assault on the World Superbike Championship in the 1990s, however. Having witnessed the spectacular recovery of the previously struggling Ducati company in the wake of its success in this worldwide race series with its global audience of possible customers, Harley wanted a piece of the action...

HARLEY-DAVIDSON VR1000

If the Café Racer had been a shock to the system of the Harley purists, the VR1000 must have given them a purple fit. In an attempt to emulate Ducati's achievements in superbike racing, all the old Harley hallmarks were thrown away, apart from the V-twin

engine configuration—and even that was changed to a 60° vee and not the company's traditional 45°!

The engine was an all-new, purpose-built 60.8 cubic inch (996cc) powerplant with liquid cooling, four valves per cylinder and twin overhead camshafts, while the frame was of twin-beam design and made from aluminium, just like the top Japanese superbikes used. Most other components were bought in, including high-quality Ohlins forks and Marchesini magnesium alloy wheels.

But despite the effort put into this radical departure from the Harley norm, the race bike failed to achieve any real racing success when it first entered the AMA Superbike series in 1994. Way down on power compared to its rivals, it wasn't until 1998/99 that the VR1000 was developed to produce a competitive 170bhp. But even in this →

HARLEY-DAVIDSON VR1000

SPECIFICATIONS

Introduced
1994
Engine
Liquid cooled
60° V-twin
four-stroke
Capacity
60 cu in (996cc)
Power
170bhp
Top speed
N/A

The even more radical Harley VR1000 racer failed to achieve its aim of success in the World Superbike series

The Firebolt has the heart and soul of a Harley-Davidson but its nonconformist attitude is a true Buell trademark

→ form it failed to cut it in domestic Superbike competition in the States.

To qualify for these competitions, motorcycles had to be street-legal, and Harley had an ingenious way of navigating around the rules to enable it to sell the VR1000 to private race teams. To save the huge expense of achieving the road-legal standard in the USA, the company had a batch of 50 'roadster' VRs registered in Poland, where it met the standard for roadgoing motorcycles. As long as they were road legal somewhere, it was within the rules!

Although a prototype street-legal version of the VR1000 was put together, it never made it to the showrooms and with no success on the track, the plug was pulled on the project in 2001. The ultimate circuit-racing Harley had failed to make it to street legal status (except in Poland!), but had carved a unique niche for itself in the history of the company.

In fact, something good was to come out of Harley's flirtation with new methods of construction. One of the original development engineers on the VR1000 project was a guy called Erik Buell, and he was to prove an instrumental figure in shaping a successful future for sports motorcycles powered by Harley-Davidson engines...

BUELL FIREBOLT XB12R

Erik Buell was a former racer who had moved on to motorcycle development and production. After working on the VR1000 project, he went on to produce his own race bikes and street-legal sportsters powered by Harley-Davidson engines.

His innovative and unconventional approach to design produced sports motorcycles with their own distinct image and attitude. Harley-Davidson picked up on this and, after first buying a 49% interest in Erik Buell's company, now own a controlling share. Buell is now essentially the sports bike arm of Harley-Davidson motorcycles.

The current Firebolt XB12R is the ultimate expression of Buell's radical design stategy. Powered by a modified version of Harley's 73 cubic inch (1199cc) Sportster engine, it is a showcase for the company's idiosyncratic engineering. The chassis is as short as a 250cc race bike, and features advanced monoshock suspension. The exhaust muffler is underslung beneath the engine and the front brake features a rim-mounted disc.

The engine may produce only 103bhp, puny compared to current superbike standards, but it is rewardingly torquey and responsive, while the Firebolt's handling has been widely praised as being right up there with the best the world can offer. This is an American motorcycle that has the character and soul of a Harley-Davidson but is as far away from that company's traditional cruiser formula as it is possible to get.

And Buell isn't the only American company breaking the cruiser mould...

A NEW AMERICAN DREAM

Fischer is a new American motorcycle company set up by ex-racer Dan Fischer. In fact it's so new its first motorcycle, the MRX, has yet to be launched →

With its exotic bodywork and unique cleft tail unit, the Fischer is another American bike that's different from the norm

"**With strong acceleration even from 150mph,**" **Suzuki's Hayabusa could eat anything else on the street for breakfast**

→ as this book goes to press.

Powered by a Korean-manufactured Hyosung 650cc V-twin motor, it will certainly not be the most powerful sports bike in the world, as this engine only produces 77bhp in stock form. It could offer the buyer excellent value for money for such an exotically-styled and exclusive machine, however, with a target price of just $8,000 (£4,250).

Moving back again to recent worldwide developments in the world of performance bikes, there have been some machines produced to satisfy the desire by some customers for much more power than the Fischer can offer.

Designed to eclipse even cutting-edge superbikes in the outright speed stakes, they have created a whole new category of motorcycles...

THE HYPERBIKES

The competition between the major Japanese motorcycle manufacturers to out-perform each other reached new heights in the late 1990s. The race was on to produce the ultimate street-legal speed machine, and Honda struck a killer blow in 1996 with its CBR1100XX Super Blackbird.

Machines such as Kawasaki's ZZ-R1100 had already established the formula of a hugely powerful engine housed in a motorcycle with roomier dimensions that offered more rider comfort and was better suited to touring than superbikes with their ever-shrinking size. The Super Blackbird took that idea and added extra speed—its aerodynamic bodywork helped to give it a potential 180mph maximum, making it the fastest production motorcycle in the world when it was launched.

It also heralded in the era of a new breed of two-wheeled machine—the hyperbike.

SUZUKI HAYABUSA

The other Japanese factories were not going to allow Honda to be top dog in the outright speed stakes for ever, and in 1999 one of them produced a machine which toppled the Super Blackbird from its lofty perch. That was the year in which Suzuki revealed the GSX1300R Hayabusa, a hyperbike capable of achieving an outrageous 190mph.

The Hayabusa's 1298cc four-cylinder engine used fuel injection and 'ram air', a system designed to feed it with a highly-pressurised charge of fuel and air mixture, to maximise power and produce a stomping 173bhp. But to better the Super Blackbird's top speed, Suzuki had to do more than just improve on the Honda's power figure of 162bhp.

At such high velocity, the science of aerodynamics becomes prevalent, with ability of an object to cut through the air as efficiently as possible being paramount for increasing top speed. So Suzuki concentrated a great deal of effort on developing the Hayabusa's ultra-streamlined bodywork to achieve its aim of producing the world's fastest production motorcycle.

The Hayabusa's astonishing performance was backed up by a very capable chassis, giving the bike light steering and great stability. With strong →

SUZUKI HAYABUSA

SPECIFICATIONS

Introduced
1999
Engine
In-line four-cylinder four-stroke
Capacity
1298cc
Power
173bhp
Top speed
190mph

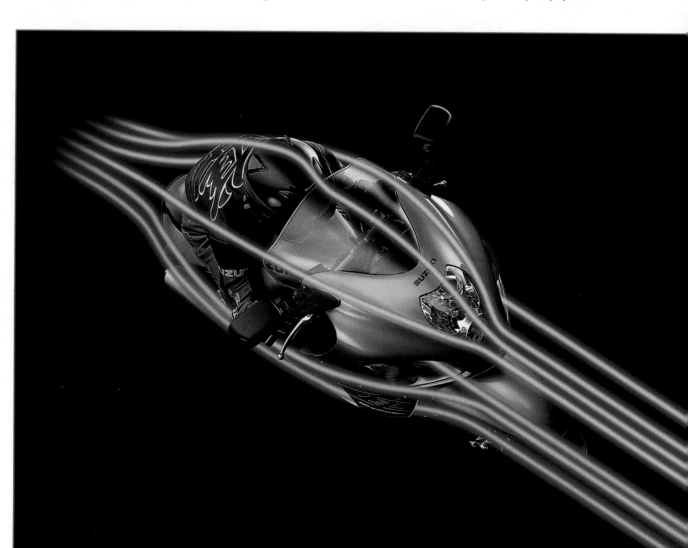

The Hayabusa's aerodynamic body work is designed to let air slip over its surface as efficiently as possible, cutting down drag and allowing a 190mph top speed

KAWASAKI ZZR1400

The ZZR1400 (or ZX-14, as it's known in the States) is currently the fastest, most powerful production bike

→ acceleration even from 150mph, the Hayabusa could eat anything else on the street for breakfast. Its robust and superbly engineered mechanicals made it a favourite for motorcycle tuners and drag racers, who managed to coax even more power and top speed from the engine.

With the advent of the Hayabusa, it seemed that the quest for speed had reached its absolute zenith, with some authorities even calling for a ban on hyperbikes and the introduction of legally-enforced limits on the power and top speed of motorcycles. So far, that has not happened, but under this threat the 'Big Four' Japanese bike manufacturers did come

to a gentleman's agreement which limited the top speed of any motorcycles they produced to 'only' 186mph. But that did not stop them attempting to better each other in the hyperbike class.

KAWASAKI ZZR1400

At the time of writing, it is Kawasaki which holds the title of world's fastest and most powerful production bike, with its ZZR1400 hyperbike (called the ZX-14 in the USA). With a 1352cc in-line four-cylinder engine producing a mind-boggling 197bhp, this machine boasts a maximum speed capabilty that nudges even closer to the 200mph mark than the

incredible Hayabusa.

An advanced aluminium monocoque chassis is used to house that beast of an engine, which also uses a ram air system to maximise power. The bodywork is designed to enhance aerodynamic efficiency, including Ferrari Testarossa-style side strakes on the fairing to channel the air in its passage over the bike at high speeds.

If we're talking bangs for your buck, this Kawasaki represents the ultimate in value for money for the serious speed freak, selling at £8995 in the UK ($11,499 in the USA). That's an incredible bargain, especially considering that it will blow the fastest Ferrari you can buy into the weeds in a drag race!

But not all riders are obsessed with the idea of owning the quickest thing on the road, and one manufacturer which has recently entered the sports bike market has a unique approach to both engineering and design

BMW GETS SPORTY

For many years BMW motorcycles were renowned for their build quality, reliability and ability to cover vast distances while maintaining high levels of rider

The R1200S is powered by BMW's most powerful 'boxer' twin engine ever, which produces 122bhp

comfort. In short, they were for old guys.

Over the last few years, however, the company has been busy trying to emulate the sporting image of its car division by producing more sports-focused motorcycles. With their highly individual styling, these bikes are still recognizably BMWs, but are aimed at the rider looking for a bike with →

Buyers of the high-tech K1200S can opt for a system which offers three electronically adjustable suspension settings

BMW R1200S

SPECIFICATIONS

Introduced
2006
Engine
Horizontally-opposed twin-cylinder four-stroke
Capacity
1170cc
Power
122bhp
Top speed
135mph

BMW K1200S

SPECIFICATIONS

Introduced
2005
Engine
In-line four-cylinder four-stroke
Capacity
1157cc
Power
165bhp
Top speed
175mph

→ improved performance and handling capabilities.

The R1200S features BMW's traditional 'boxer' engine, its horizontally-opposed twin cylinders arranged across the chassis. The boxer has been a staple ingredient in BMW motorcycles for many decades, but the version which powers the R1200S is the most powerful ever, at 122bhp.

As with all of the company's high-capacity bikes, the power is transferred to the rear wheel by a maintenance-free shaft drive. Instead of a pair of forks to deal with the front suspension, BMW's patented Telelever system is fitted.

By BMW standards, this is a stripped-down sportster, weighing in at 190kg (419lb) and capable of 135mph, but it can still be loaded with optional safety and luxury features such as a trip computer and anti-lock brakes, a feature long available on cars but only offered for motorcycles fairly recently.

The K1200S is powered by a four-cylinder engine, producing 165bhp and giving this 226kg (498lb) motorcycle a 175mph top speed capability. BMW's appliance of unique technology is even more to the forefront in the K1200S. The front suspension is BMW's own 'Duolever' system, a double-wishbone arrangement with a solid fork, designed to improve stability at speed and reaction to bumps.

The K1200S's optional 'ESA' system offers three electronically-adjustable suspension modes which can be selected by a handlebar-mounted button. This enables the rider to select 'comfort' mode, to soften the suspension for long trips, 'normal' mode for everyday riding or 'sports' setting for a blast on a favourite twisty road.

The usual range of BMW options is available, including everything from heated hand grips to anti-lock brakes and a trip computer. This is one sports bike on which the rider doesn't have to forego the creature comforts of a large touring machine.

The K1200S is a measure of how far motorcycle technology has been developed in the past few decades. The guys who put together the GSX-R750 back in 1985 would be absolutely amazed!

Harley-Davidson DESTROYER

The outrageous Destroyer was a racer that could be bought from a Harley dealer and taken straight to the drag strip

Being able to walk into a dealership to buy a fully-built professional-level drag racing motorcycle sounds like the ultimate speed-freak biker's dream. But Harley-Davidson made this fantasy come true when it thrust the Destroyer onto an unsuspecting public in 2005.

The VRXSE Screamin' Eagle V-Rod Destroyer, to give it its full name, was a single-minded monster designed with one purpose alone: to cover a quarter-mile in the quickest possible time. With no concessions made to street legality, this was a bike built solely for competition on the drag strip.

Modern day drag racing originated in the United States, but is now also popular in Europe and other parts of the world. In a drag race, two competitors line up side by side on a straight, quarter-mile strip. As soon as the start lights give the riders the signal to go, they accelerate as hard as they can, aiming to complete the measured distance in the shortest possible time.

Ultimate straight-line acceleration is the name of the game for drag bikes, and building one is a very expensive business. The Destroyer's price tag may have seemed high at £20,000 in the UK ($31,249 in the USA), but compared to the cost of having such a machine custom-built it was a bargain.

A product of Harley-Davidson's Custom Vehicle Operations department, set up to create individualised versions of existing Harley models

PHOTOGRAPHY: GARETH HARFORD/GHP

www.blac

to be sold direct to the public, the Destroyer was loosely based on the company's V-Rod street bike. Of coufrse, the components had been highly modified to produce a machine capable of covering a quarter mile from standstill in a blistering 9.5 seconds in the hands of a professional drag racer.

The liquid-cooled engine of 79 cubic inches (1300cc) displacement was fitted with forged high-compression pistons, modified cylinder heads with high-lift camshafts and special valves and springs to make fuel and exhaust gases flow more quickly through the engine. This process is assisted by a two-into-one ceramic-coated exhaust system.

All these modifications add up to around a 165bhp power figure and made the Destroyer by far the fastest-accelerating motorcycle ever to be offered for sale by Harley-Davidson dealerships—and the quickest ready-built 'turnkey' bike in the world during its limited production lifetime.

Changing gears is dealt with by a handlebar-operated 'air shifter' which uses compressed air to help the rider select gears in the quickest possible time. The transmission was specially built for the Destroyer, with drive via the same chain used on championship-winning drag racers.

The rear end of the Destroyer is the most visually striking, with its massive seven-inch wide Dunlop slick tyre and long 'wheelie bar'. Like all drag bikes, this Harley unleashes enough power on full throttle to flip the bike clean over, with the wheelie bar's job being to stop that happening.

The Destroyer was built in very limited numbers. We're talking a three-figure production run, of which less than 10 were shipped to the UK, ensuring that the quickest production Harley ever made is also one of the rarest.

HARLEY-DAVIDSON DESTROYER

SPECIFICATIONS

Introduced
2005
Engine
Liquid cooled
60° V-twin
four-stroke
Capacity
79 cu in (1300cc)
Power
165bhp
Standing quarter mile
Sub-nine seconds

With its low attitude and long wheelie bar, the Destroyer has classic drag racer looks, and it ain't just cosmetic. This beast is capable of sub-nine second times for the quarter-mile

OFF-ROAD/SUPERMOTO MOTORCYCLES

BMW HP2

OFF-ROAD & SUPERMOTO *Motorcycles*

Riding a motorcycle off-road is a totally different proposition to riding on the highway. Bikes designed to be ridden through dirt, sand and rocks have to be as rugged as the terrain they tackle. Supermotos are basically off-road bikes adapted to race on circuits which feature both asphalt and off-road sections

The off-road motorcycle is a completely different breed to the machines designed to pound the highway. The ability to deal with all terrains is paramount, as is toughness and resilience. These machines must be able to handle riding through dirt, rocks, sand, water and anything else the land can throw at them.

The development of off-road bikes to fit this purpose has led to some specific characteristics. To handle the extra shocks of riding over rugged terrain, long-travel suspension is essential to soak up bumps and heavy landings. This has led to the classic 'stacked up' look of today's dirt bikes, with very long front forks and raised rear suspension which also allow for plenty of ground clearance beneath the engine to prevent damage by rocks.

Another distinctive feature of the off-road two-wheeler is knobbly tires. Deeply-treaded with big blocks of rubber, they are designed to give maximum traction over loose and rough surfaces. As well as being purely functional, they also add to the ➤

APRILIA RXV 450

→ distinctively rugged look of the classic dirt bike.

The supermoto is a more recent hybrid of the off-road motorcycle. This type of bike was initially designed specifically for competitions which include asphalt and off-road sections; it is a kind of racing that originated in Europe and has rapidly gained in popularity over the last decade. On the back of this, more manufacturers have produced street-legal supermotos to satisfy public demand.

APRILIA RXV 450

Aprilia has a proud racing history and has built its reputation on successfully converting its race bikes for use by the general public. The RXV is the latest expression of that process, being a street-legal version of the company's current enduro racers.

At the heart of the bike is Aprilia's all-new 449cc 77° V-twin two-stroke engine—a radical departure for an enduro bike, it is a high-revving power plant which revs to 13,000rpm and puts out around 65bhp. An even more powerful 549cc version is also planned for production.

The RXV not only has the power to make it an exciting ride both on and off-road, it also looks incredibly cool. Slim, light and compact, it has that purposeful 'race-ready' look that has characterised

Aprilia's beautiful RXV enduro bike is powered by the company's all-new and extremely compact high-revving 449cc V-twin engine

many of Aprilia's bikes. The company also produces a supermoto version of the bike, called the SXV, which has an equally impressive pedigree as a race bike; it features bigger forks, sticky road tires and more powerful brakes.

BMW R1200GS ADVENTURE

The Adventure is massive in every respect. Its huge size gives it impressive road presence, while its considerable weight, at 256kg (564lb) fully fuelled and tall seat height make it a serious hunk of bike to for anyone to handle.

Its abilities as an all-terrain machine are equally impressive. This is the latest development of the bike which took Hollywood actor Ewan McGregor and pal Charley Boorman right round the world in their famous adventure which was the subject of the 'Long Way Round' book and television series, taking on everything from rutted Mongolian dirt tracks to the highways of North America.

The Adventure is powered by an 1170cc version of BMW's venerable flat-twin 'boxer' engine, which puts the emphasis on torque rather than outright power. It produces 100bhp, but more important is its low-down and mid-range grunt.

Another impressive characteristic is the bike's ➔

SPECIFICATIONS

Introduced
2006
Engine
Oil/air-cooled flat-twin four-stroke
Capacity
1170cc
Power
100bhp
Seat height
915mm (36in)

BMW's R1200GS Adventure is a great bike for riders who like to cover massive mileages, with excellent on and off-road abilities

fuel range. With a massive 33-litre (7.26-gallon) gas tank, over 300 miles can be covered on one fill-up, adding to the Adventure's long-distance abilities. Excellent weather protection and great levels of comfort afforded by the upright riding position and well-padded seat also help to make it a consummate mile-eater, with options such as heated handgrips and ABS brakes making it a true all-weather and all-terrain machine.

BMW HP2

While BMW's Adventure is an all-rounder that is as happy on a highway as it is on a dirt track, the company's HP2 is a hardcore off-roader with none of the creature comforts that make its stable-mate such a comfortable companion on the road.

Although, like the Adventure, it is essentially based on the standard road-going R1200GS, the HP2 has been developed by BMW Motorrad's new High Performance department as a serious off-road racer. The bike uses the 1170cc version of the company's long-standing 'boxer' flat twin, tuned to produce 105bhp, but the rest of the machine is far from traditional BMW practice.

The tubular steel space frame was developed from years of competition in the gruelling Paris-Dakar rally and, unlike other big-capacity BMWs, the HP2 uses conventional forks to deal with →

BMW HP2

SPECIFICATIONS

Introduced
2005
Engine
Oil/air-cooled flat-twin four-stroke
Capacity
1170cc
Power
105bhp
Top speed
320mm (12.6in)

Developed as a hardcore off-road racer, the HP2 has acquitted itself well in competition, with a podium finish in America's arduous Baja 1000 desert race

KTM 990 ADVENTURE S

SPECIFICATIONS

Introduced
2005
Engine
Liquid-cooled
75° V-twin
four-stroke
Capacity
999cc
Power
96bhp
Ground clearance
316mm (12.4in)

→ front suspension. There is a specially-developed spring-less air shock absorber at the rear.

With successful campaigns in numerous off-road events worldwide, the HP2 has proved its worth as a competition machine. This ultimate off-roader has a high-end price, at £11,995 in the UK ($21,000 in the USA) and is made in limited numbers.

KTM 990 ADVENTURE S

Reflecting KTM's unparalleled success in what is commonly regarded as the toughest and most dangerous motor race in the world, the Paris-Dakar rally, the Adventure S comes emblazoned with 'Dakar' graphics. The bike is a version of the company's standard Adventure model, with a more serious off-road focus than its all-rounder namesake, and the paint job is not the only difference between the two variants.

The 'S' has more suspension travel than the standard Adventure, enabling it to tackle even tougher terrain. It is powered by the same engine, though—the latest 999cc version of KTM's excellent LC8 motor also seen in the Austrian company's Super Duke naked bike and RC8 superbike. Although

KTM's 990 Adventure S celebrates the company's many successes in the toughest off-road race in the world, the Dakar Rally, and makes a seriously capable road bike, too

it is detuned to 96bhp when used in the Adventure, it is still a worthy engine to power this street-legal machine which celebrates the company's success in the toughest race in the world.

KTM DUKE

One of the first production supermotos built by an established firm, KTM's original 1994 Duke was a typical example of this new type of motorcycle. Supermotos are closely related to off-road machines, with long-travel suspension, tall and narrow seats and flat bars. Like most off-road competition machines, they tend to have single-cylinder engines.

The Duke II, which was launched in 1999, was powered by a 625cc version of the original Duke's 609cc engine producing 54bhp. The original version had the typical thumping throb of a single-cylinder motor, although the Duke II featured improved carburetors which made power delivery smoother and twin underseat exhaust cans which gave it a slightly more civilised sound.

A popular bike with urban commuters due to its great manoeuvrability through traffic and its lofty seating position which gave a great view of the ➔

PHOTOGRAPHY: H MITTERBAUER

KTM DUKE

SPECIFICATIONS

Introduced
1994
Engine
Liquid-cooled single-cylinder four-stroke
Capacity
625cc
Power
54bhp
Ground clearance
250mm (9.8in)

The Duke was around for 11 years, helping to blaze a trail for the new breed of supermoto machines. This is the Duke II, which was finally phazed out in 2005

Ducati
HYPERMOTARD

The Hypermotard should make the transition from concept bike to production in 2007, hopefully with this superb styling intact

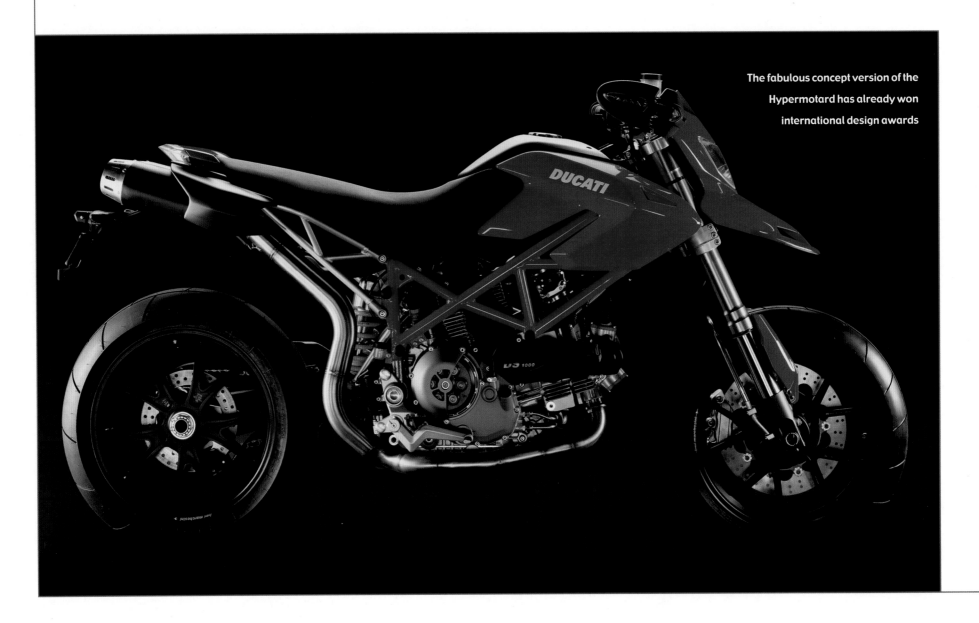

The fabulous concept version of the Hypermotard has already won international design awards

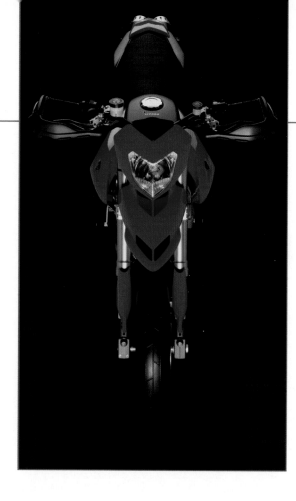

DUCATI HYPERMOTARD

SPECIFICATIONS

Introduced
2007 (planned)
Engine
Air-cooled
90° V-twin
four-stroke
Capacity
992cc
Power
100bhp
Weight
175kg (385lb)

Cool features include indicators that can be folded back to act as hand guards, as can be seen above

*I*f the production version of the Ducati Hypermotard looks anywhere near as cool as the concept bike shown on these pages, it will be the sexiest supermoto on the planet.

First shown in 2005 at Milan, it wowed both Ducati fans and the press, being awarded 'Best of Show' and 'Best Bike for 2005' by the Motorcycle Design Association. The overwhelming response to the concept bike made Ducati move to put the bike into production as quickly as possible.

The Hypermotard shares the same basic chassis as the company's Multistrada multi-purpose bike but features a new alloy rear subframe to help keep weight down. Suspension is state-of-the-art, with huge 50mm upside-down Marzocchi forks and an Ohlins remote-reservoir rear shock.

Powered by the latest version of Ducati's air-cooled 992cc 1000DS engine, also from the Multistrada, the Hypermotard is expected to have around 100bhp and weigh about 175kg (385lb). The engine's magnesium engine covers are designed to reduce weight, while a slipper-type racing clutch allows for aggressive downshifting.

Gorgeous, ultra-light forged and machined Marchesini racing wheels are paired with a single radial-mounted Brembo brake caliper gripping a 320mm disc up front and a 240mm disc at the rear. Cool design features include folding indicators that double as handguards.

The Hypermotard has been subjected to a thoroughly modern and democratic appraisal process, with a dedicated website set up for Ducati fans to engage in an open debate about the pros and cons of the design. In an indication of how important this model is for the company, Ducati's President Federico Minoli has taken personal responsibility for the Hypermotard project.

This is a machine that has the kind of sex appeal that marked out Ducati's iconic 916 (see 'Sports Motorcycles' section) as an instant classic. If the processes involved in converting it into a production bike are kind to the Hypermotard, it has all the hallmarks of a big success.

Whether Ducati can carry it off will only become clear in the spring of 2007, when the bike is planned to become available in dealerships.

→ road ahead over the top of cars, the Duke's distinctive style also cut a dash in city streets.

Although the Duke was never manufactured in great numbers and was discontinued in 2005, it earns its place in this book as one of the early trailblazers of the supermoto style.

Over the last decade, the supermoto craze has developed in Europe, with many race series springing up. Supermoto racing takes part on circuits which combine two different elements: a 'road racing' section on asphalt and an off-road section on dirt usually with motocross-style jumps.

Supermoto racers have developed a distinct cornering style for the asphalt sections—rather than keeping their inside foot on the footpeg, they stretch their inside forwards to allow the bike to achieve as acute an angle of lean as possible.

KTM has 'kept the faith' with street-legal supermoto motorcycles for longer than most manufacturers and still produces some of the coolest and most able machines out there.

KTM 950 SUPERMOTO

This is basically a supermoto version of KTM's 950 Adventure (the predecessor to the 990 Adventure featured earlier in this section) which, with the 942cc version of the company's acclaimed LC8 V-twin engine, combines the riding position of an off-roader with sports bike performance.

The whole package is developed with light weight and performance in mind. That LC8 engine weighs just 58kg, the lightest twin in the 1,000cc class. The chromium-molybdenum frame, modified from that of the Adventure, comes in at a featherlight 11 kg. With a steeper steering head angle and a shorter wheelbase, it gives the chassis a sharp and sporty edge, with quality WP suspension that can cut it on country tracks as well as the road.

The 17-inch wheels from the 990 Super Duke allow the fitting of sticky sports bike tires, while 305mm front discs with radial calipers and master cylinder, backed up with a 240mm rear disc and →

The 690 Supermoto's distinctive
upswept pipes echo the style of the
company's all-conquering rally bikes

→ two-piston caliper combine to give superbike levels of stopping power. For riders who love to do wheelies, stoppies and slide the back wheel into corners, the 950 Supermoto is hard to beat.

KTM 690 SUPERMOTO

There seems to be no stopping KTM as 2006 draws to a close. The company is going hell-for-leather with its assault on the street bike market, kicking out hot new machines which boost its cool image by doing things differently from the pack.

The 690 Supermoto keeps up the momentum with an entirely newly-developed 690 Supermoto due for release in 2007. Driven by an all-new fuel-injected single-cylinder engine with 63hp and a new six-speed transmission, this bike cannot fail to make a big impression on image-conscious city slickers.

Weighing in at only 152kg (335lb) and with adjustable suspension and high-performance brakes, this bike fills the gap left in the KTM range by the dropping of the Duke (see earlier in this section) in 2005 and looks to move the single-cylinder supermoto concept to the next level.

The standout visual feature is the twin upswept exhaust pipes, similar in style to those used on KTM's all-conquering Dakar Rally racers. If the 690 Supermoto proves as big a success as its racers, KTM really is destined for a big sales winner..

With sports bike levels of performance and an off-road riding position, the 950 Supermoto is a potent combination

PHOTOGRAPHY: KTM & H MITTERBAUER

SPECIFICATIONS

KTM 690 SUPERMOTO

Introduced
2007 (planned)
Engine
Liquid cooled single-cylinder four-stroke
Capacity
690cc
Power
63bhp
Top speed
N/A

SPECIFICATIONS

KTM 950 SUPERMOTO

Introduced
2005
Engine
Liquid-cooled 75° V-twin four-stroke
Capacity
942cc
Power
98bhp
Top speed
137mph

NAKED MOTORCYCLES

KTM SUPERDUKE

PHOTOGRAPHY: F LHE

NAKED *Motorcycles*

In the naked motorcycle, the component parts are exposed for the eye to see. The only wind protection may be a small headlamp fairing, as displayed by the KTM Superduke on the left. The owners of these machines really like to feel the rush of the wind past their bodies as they ride, and are happy to forsake a full fairing for the sake of unfettered style

With their back-to-basics charm, uncluttered with the full fairings of sports bikes or tourers, naked bikes are a passport to experiencing the raw sensations of riding a motorcycle. With minimal wind protection, and often none at all, these machines put the rider right out there in the elements where the full force of air rushing by can be felt.

For this reason, naked bikes give the rider a greater sensation of speed than those which offer greater protection from the wind blast. This, combined with the fact that they are more physically demanding to ride at high speed, means that they are a popular choice for bikers who have grown out of the phase of thrashing around on sports bikes and want to slow it down a little.

Many riders who fear that their sports bikes will get them into trouble with the law have also opted for nakeds in an attempt to avoid being fined or losing their license for speeding.

For others, it's simply a question of style. In the naked bike, all the major components are on show—especially the engine, and being able to see the power unit in all its glory is a big deal for a lot of bikers. Whether the styling of the rest of the bike is wild and outrageous like the KTM Superduke ➔

A prime example of the naked muscle bike,
Suzuki's GSX1400 has its stomping great
1402cc engine proudly on full display

→ or more traditional like the Suzuki GSX1400, the fact that you can see the pumping heart of the motorcycle is of paramount importance.

SUZUKI GSX1400

Suzuki's GSX1400 is an example of a traditional naked motorcycle which delivers the raw ingredients of a bike with a no-frills attitude. There are no unnecessary add-ons, what you get is a big engine on full display with a familiar, tried-and-tested suspension layout and no fancy single-sided swingarms or the like.

It is an example of a dying breed of motorcycle, the muscle bike, with the emphasis on that huge 1402cc in-line four-cylinder engine which has truckloads of sheer brute power and pumps out 104bhp. It is a big old beast which appeals to the hairy-chested macho biker who has no interest in race replicas wrapped in plastic fairings. The guys who ride these machines hanker for the purer motorcycling pleasures of a bygone age.

That big engine, Suzuki's biggest four-cylinder unit and the largest-capacity power unit currently used in a traditionally-styled muscle bike, has to haul 229kg (498lb) of motorcycle around (as well as the weight of its rider) so it is tuned to produce effortless pulling power rather than having to be revved hard to give its best.

The GSX1400 is quite literally a dying breed. Despite being fitted with the latest dual throttle-valve electronic fuel injection, the bike's engine will not meet new European emissions regulations, so the bike pictured left, the Final Edition, will be the last of the breed for the UK market.

YAMAHA V-MAX

The V-Max is an eccentric motorcycle that refuses to fit comfortably into any particular category. Its styling and riding position are nearer to the classic American cruiser than anything else, a reflection of the fact that Yamaha's original intention was to build a bike specifically for the US market. However, its

engine, which is the truly unique part of the motorcycle, is much more powerful than those found in the traditional cruiser. A V4 giving a mighty 145bhp, it seemed more suited to powering a sports bike than anything else. What is not in doubt, though, is that it is a naked motorcycle, with no concession to wind protection.

The American public loved it when it was first put on sale in 1985. Inspired by the bikes that took part in illicit street drag racing in the United States, it was built with one simple aim: to be the motorcycle with the fastest straight-line acceleration available to the general public.

To achieve this aim, the 1198cc engine employs a clever and unique trick called V-Boost. When engine revs reach 6,500, an intake valve allows each of the four cylinders to be fed fuel by two carburettors rather than one, giving the serious 'kick in the pants' power boost that is the V-Max's trademark. This helps the bike to cover a quarter-mile from a standstill in under 11 seconds, an impressive feat →

The V-Max's unique V-Boost system gives a serious kick at over 6,500rpm, giving it very quick straight-line acceleration

SUZUKI GSX1400

SPECIFICATIONS

Introduced
2002
Engine
In-line
four-cylinder
four-stroke
Capacity
1402cc
Power
104bhp
Top speed
130mph

YAMAHA V-MAX

SPECIFICATIONS

Introduced
1985
Engine
Liquid-cooled
70° V4
four-stroke
Capacity
1198cc
Power
145bhp
Top speed
127mph

Introduced
2006
Engine
Liquid-cooled
90° V-twin
four-stroke
Capacity
998cc
Power
130bhp
Top speed
135mph

Ducati Monster
S4RS

The most powerful and exclusive of Ducati's well-established and eternally popular Monster range

Ducati's success in the World Superbike championships in the early '90s may have increased the formerly struggling Italian company's profile, but it was one model which was to reap the financial rewards of its rebirth of cool: the Monster. With its naked styling exposing the trademark Ducati V-twin motor and with easygoing practicality to back up the Italian good looks, the Monster was a worldwide hit.

The model has now been in production for 13

The Monster S4RS has the engine from Ducati's 999 superbike giving it 130bhp, a serious amount of power for a naked motorcycle

years, and although there have been a lot of changes and developments in that time, the Monster is still the same machine at heart.

The current top-of-the-range Monster is the S4RS pictured here. The main thing that sets it apart from lesser Monsters is its 'Testastretta' engine from Ducati's 999 superbike, which endows the S4RS with 130bhp. The bike's steel trellis frame has had to be strengthened to enable it to take the extra power.

Top quality Ohlins suspension is fitted front and rear, giving a finer range of adjustment and reducing weight compared to lesser Monsters. Using carbon-fiber components such as engine covers has achieved further weight reduction.

And if the standard S4RS Monster isn't ultimate enough for you, there is a way of making this bike perform to an even higher standard. It comes in the form of the official race kit offered by Ducati for this model.

This hop-up kit consists of a big-bore full-race exhaust from famous Italian firm Termignoni, a free-flow air filter and an uprated electronic control unit to alter the engine mapping. The kit brings an extra 18bhp to the party, along with a lot more noise. That means 148bhp and a machine which can boast the booming exhausts that are the calling card of the classic Ducati, rather than the muted, strangled and emission-regulations-dictated note of the standard machine.

Also, as the S4RS is powered by an engine from Ducati's 999 range, you can take your pick from the whole catalogue of tuning parts offered for this particular engine, including high-compression pistons, a slipper clutch and racing camshafts. So the sky's the limit with the S4RS, with ample opportunity to blow much more than the £9495 ($14,995 in the USA) asking price for the standard bike in the UK.

→ for a straight-out-of-the-crate motorcycle. No wonder the V-Max is such a cult motorcycle revered by speed freaks and street drag racers.

CAGIVA V-RAPTOR

Here we have another quirky motorcycle, this time from Italian company Cagiva. The V-Raptor came in two sizes, both being powered by Suzuki V-twin engines: a 645cc version with 70bhp capable of a 124mph top speed and a 996cc model producing 116bhp with a 136mph top speed.

A less extravagantly-styled version of the bike, simply called the Raptor, was also available with the same choice of engine capacities. It was the looks of the V-Raptor which made it stand out from the crowd, however. The bizarre front-end styling gave it an extraterrestrial look, like something out of one of the Alien films.

Cagiva, in common with many fellow Italian →

CAGIVA V-RAPTOR 1000

SPECIFICATIONS

Introduced
2000
Engine
Liquid-cooled 90° V-twin four-stroke
Capacity
996cc
Power
116bhp
Top speed
136mph

The V-Raptor's quirky Italian style was wrapped around a Suzuki V-twin engine

The Speed Triple T509 of 1997 introduced the current model's distinctive tubular frame, but its 107bhp 955cc engine breathed via a single low-level exhaust

→ bike manufacturers, was subject to its fair share of financial crises, so the Raptor has never been built in great numbers and remains a cult motorcycle.

TRIUMPH SPEED TRIPLE

After years of decline, the British motorcycle industry was dealt a body blow when Triumph, one of its most famous manufacturers, went bust in 1983. But one man, English construction multi-millionaire John Bloor, had a mind to keep the marque alive, and bought the name.

Bloor spent eight years secretly developing a range of new Triumph motorcycles, which were brought out in 1991 to initial success. Building on this, the new Triumph company produced its most inspired model in 1994—the Speed Triple. With its aggressive stance and 97bhp, 885cc three-cylinder engine, it recalled the company's halcyon days of the '50s and '60s—the time of ton-up boys and Triumph's domination of the motorcycle market.

But this was not an exercise in rose-tinted nostalgia, it was a thoroughly modern motorcycle, and one which had true longevity. A completely restyled version came out in 1997, with even more aggressive styling influenced by the European cult of the 'streetfighter' motorcycle, which saw bikes stripped down to their raw basics and often fitted with aggressive-looking twin headlamps up front

A further redesign in 2005 accentuated the bike's compact, muscular form further with upswept stubby exhaust cans. Aided by a bigger 1050cc engine giving 112bhp and a black-painted frame, the Speed Triple emerged as the Pit Bull Terrier of the motorcycle world, a hard case that could really →

TRIUMPH SPEED TRIPLE 1050

SPECIFICATIONS

Introduced
2005
Engine
In-line three-cylinder four-stroke
Capacity
1050cc
Power
128bhp
Top speed
154mph

The latest Speed Triple 1050 (below) looks as purposeful as a sawn-off shotgun with its twin stubby high-level pipes

APRILIA TUONO

SPECIFICATIONS

Introduced
2002
Engine
LIquid-cooled
60° V-twin
four-stroke
Capacity
998cc
Power
133bhp
Top speed
155mph

→ mix it in the dog-eat-dog world of the urban jungle. The Speed Triple can still cut it, even after 12 years out on the streets.

APRILIA TUONO

2002 saw the unveiling of Aprilia's version of the naked motorcycle, the Tuono. Basically a version of the Italian company's RSV Mille superbike stripped of its fairing and with high bars fitted, it was available initially in a limited edition of only 200 to gauge reaction to a naked Aprilia. These sold out within days of being put on sale and convinced Aprilia that there was an ongoing market for the model.

For 2003, a full production model was introduced, using the same 998cc V-twin engine that powered the RSV Mille, but slightly detuned to produce 126bhp. The Tuono has been in production ever since, with subsequent versions becoming ever more extreme in terms of both performance and styling. The Tuono is certainly a bike for the extrovert with its flashy paint job and in-your-face looks.

The Tuono R is now the name given to the base model Tuono, which for 2006 has the engine from the latest version of the RSV Mille, detuned to →

Eye-popping looks and eye-watering acceleration make the latest Aprilia Tuono R the perfect bike for the speed freak who doesn't want to go unnoticed

MV AGUSTA BRUTALE 910R

MV Agusta
BRUTALE

The name says it all. This is one brutally aggressive bike with incredible performance and superb attention to detail

SPECIFICATIONS

Introduced
2006
Engine
In-line
four-cylinder
four-stroke
Capacity
909cc
Power
144bhp
Top speed
160mph

The Brutale isn't just an MV Agusta F4 superbike stripped of its clothes. It has distinctive features that are unique to the Brutale, such as the headlight shape and the pair of low-level exhaust pipes

The Brutale 910R is a naked
bike that handles like a racer

The idea of stripping the fairing from MV Agusta's drop-dead gorgeous F4 superbike (see 'Exotic Motorcycles') may seem like heresy, but it results in the most strikingly aggressive naked motorcycle around, the Brutale.

And as master motorcycle craftsman Massimo Tamburini has designed both machines, the latter bike is a truly cohesive interpretation of the former. It is so much more than just a naked F4 with high handlebars, with the Brutale having unique features at either end.

The headlight is a distinctively unique shape and the F4's trademark array of four exhaust pipes exiting from under the tail unit has been transformed into twin lower-level side pipes. The remainder of the Brutale is just as exquisitely detailed as its superbike forebear.

First released with the 749cc in-line four-cylinder power unit from the original F4 750, with slight detuning to produce 127bhp, the current Brutale packs a 909cc development of that engine, giving an even more impressive 136bhp.

The ultimate Brutale, the 910R pictured here, ups that power figure to 144bhp, thanks to a hand-polished cylinder head and new inlet ducts to let the motor breathe more easily. The package also includes a titanium full-race exhaust system.

Suspension is also upgraded on the 910R compared to the standard 910, with fully-adjustable 50mm Marzocchi forks up front and a new fully-adjustable Sachs single shock absorber at the rear.

The stiffening effect of these suspension improvements give the Brutale 910R handling that can show the very best mass-produced Japanese superbikes how it should be done.

Bigger discs with radially-mounted calipers rein in the extra performance, with Pirelli's sticky Super Corsa tyres transmitting those accelerative and decelerative forces through to the road.

The MV Agusta Brutale 910R has to be the ultimate naked motorcycle in terms of style, exclusivity, performance and price. Whether it is worth £12,500 ($19,500 in the USA) is a matter for you and your bank manager to discuss...

→ give more low-down response and a power figure of 133bhp. There is even a race-inspired version of the bike, named the Factory, which takes the standard Tuono R and adds a list of exotic components designed to increase performance and lose weight for maximum effect on the track.

Along with a special paint job, there are forged aluminum OZ wheels which are 2.5kg (5.5lb) lighter than the stock rims, plus a carbon-fiber bellypan, side panels, fender and clutch and brake master cylinder protectors. The whole thing is powered by the engine from Aprilia's RSV1000R superbike, giving a power boost to 139bhp compared to the standard Tuono's 133bhp.

The Tuono Factory is one special naked motorcycle, and it comes with a special price: £9499 in the UK ($14,000 in the USA).

NAKED FRENZY

The first half-dozen years of the 21st century has seen an explosion of the market for naked motorcycles, especially in Europe. This is where the whole trend started, when street bikers started stripping the fairings off their bikes, forsaking long-distance practicality and weather protection in the search for a harder, rawer, stripped-down style.

This craze for creating custom 'streetfighters' became so big that the major motorcycle manufacturers started to sit up and take notice, producing their own interpretations of the naked bike theme. That included the Japanese factories, which were just as keen as anyone else to capitalise on this emerging trend.

It has to be said, however, that the majority of the Japanese-produced versions of streetfighters have lacked the imagination and styling flamboyance of either their European counterparts or Buell, the one American brand to get in on the naked action.

Machines such as Honda's Hornet 900, Kawasaki's Z1000 and Yamaha's Fazer 1000 ticked all the boxes, but none of them can truly be described as an 'ultimate' naked motorcycle. One bike that →

BENELLI TNT

SPECIFICATIONS

Introduced
2004
Engine
In-line
three-cylinder
four-stroke
Capacity
1131cc
Power
135bhp
Top speed
150mph

The TNT Titanium is the most expensive and exclusive of Benelli's range of naked bikes

→ emerged from a resurgent Italian firm in 2004 can certainly lay claim to that description, with a style and attitude that the mass-produced Japanese machines could only dream of...

BENELLI TNT

Appropriately named after the abbreviation for Trinitrotoluene, a type of high explosive material, the TNT blasted onto the scene with a visual presence that could blow your eyeballs clean out of their sockets. The mass of intestinal pipes and tubes and huge dragonfly's-eye headlamps combined to give it the look of a huge, dissected insect.

This was naked bike styling taken to the max, but although the bike was manufactured by the recently revived Italian firm Benelli, the designer was an Englishman by the name of Andrew Morton.

The starting point for the TNT was Benelli's Tornado superbike, although the company stressed that the TNT was very much its own entity, rather than just a Tornado stripped of its fairing.

The Tornado's in-line three-cylinder engine was heavily modified for use in the TNT, with the main revision being the extension of the pistons' stroke (the distance that each piston moves from the bottom to the top of its travel within the engine's cylinders). By extending this length from the Tornado's 49.2mm to 62mm, the TNT's engine capacity was raised from 898cc to 1131cc.

Although capacity was raised, power was down

from the Tornado's 143bhp to 135bhp, with the TNT's engine tuned to major on low-down and mid-range response compared to the superbike's high-revving nature.

Another major feature that was changed in the Tornado's transition into a naked streetfighter was the location of the radiator. One of the Tornado's most distinctive features was its underseat radiator with attendant twin cooling fans mounted in the tail unit. The TNT dispensed with this arrangement in favour of twin radiators mounted to the side of the engine's cylinder heads. With no fairing to restrict the airflow to this area, this was an ideal location and enabled the use of a single underseat exhaust pipe to give the bike a more streamlined rear end.

Since the introduction of the original TNT, a series of exotic variants have been introduced, including Sport and Café Racer versions. The most exclusive is the Titanium model pictured here, with liberal use of carbon-fiber, a titanium exhaust system and fully-adjustable suspension.

In common with all TNTs introduced from 2005 on, the Titanium also features a dash-mounted button which allows the rider to select between two different engine settings: full power or reduced power for better control in poor traction situations.

SUZUKI B-KING

First shown at the Tokyo Show of 2001, the B-King caused a sensation with its combination of →

SPECIFICATIONS

SUZUKI B-KING

Introduced
2007 (planned)
Engine
In-line
four-cylinder
four-stroke
Capacity
1298cc
Power
Up to 175bhp
Top speed
N/A

Suzuki has finally decided to put its Hayabusa-engined B-King (below and left) into production

→ outrageous styling and the promise of awesome power. The engine in this concept bike was the power unit from the company's Hayabusa hyperbike. Not only that, a supercharger was fitted to give the already awesomely powerful engine even more go.

As the Hayabusa produces 175bhp in stock form, there was the distinct possibility of increasing that by up to 50% thanks to the supercharger, with a monstrous figure of 240bhp being bandied about.

The rest of the motorcycle featured typical concept bike add-ons such as an integrated advanced computer system, self-diagnosis systems, advanced telemetry which could use a mobile phone for remote maintenance and even a GPS-based weather warning system. In short, lots of fantasy features that didn't have a cat in hell's chance of making it to a production motorcycle just yet.

The point was, though, that Suzuki seemed serious about producing a striking naked bike with Hayabusa power, and that was enough to get the press and the public salivating. The motorcycle world held its breath in preparation for the appearance of the most powerful naked street bike ever produced... and waited... and waited.

Only now, after five years of prevarication, has Suzuki announced its decision to put the B-King into production. After dipping its toe tentatively in the water in 2006 with the introduction of the GSR600, a middleweight naked bike with watered-down B-King styling, the company has finally decided to take the plunge by including the B-King in its model line-up for 2007.

Hopefully, we will then see the final result of one of the most lengthy build-ups that any model of motorcycle has ever had. Suzuki has actually displayed the finished version of the bike at shows (see previous page), demonstrating that the B-King's styling should be almost as striking as the original concept machine .

However, despite the fact that the bike will still be powered by the stupendously powerful Hayabusa engine, it will no longer be featuring a →

Yamaha
MT-01

If you're looking for the naked motorcycle with the largest capacity engine, look no further, this is the one

YAMAHA MT-01

SPECIFICATIONS

Introduced
2005
Engine
Air-cooled
48° V-twin
four-stroke
Capacity
1670cc
Power
90bhp
Top speed
130mph

With its monstrous engine, heavy metal styling and rocket-launcher exhaust pipes, the MT-01 looks like some exaggerated comic book creation that should be ridden by Batman or Judge Dredd. But this is not a fantasy concept bike, it is a real motorcycle that can be bought in Yamaha dealerships—although only in Europe, as the company's US division does not import the bike officially.

Part sports bike, part cruiser, part naked muscle bike, this is a strange mutant machine powered by the biggest V-twin engine ever made by Yamaha. The 1670cc air-cooled unit is based on the power plant of the successful US-only cruiser the Road Star Warrior. Modifications to the 48° V-twin engine include a new lightweight crankshaft assembly to give instant pickup and rapid acceleration, to achieve Yamaha's stated aim of making the MT-01's engine more responsive than the lazy-revving version in its cruiser cousin.

The five-speed gearbox has fairly high ratios for a relaxed riding feel, while the chassis was newly designed with the intention of giving that impressive engine maximum exposure. The Yamaha engineers came up with a minimalist design that was also intended to give the bike good handling characteristics. The whole main frame is weld-free, with its components bolted together—that includes the engine itself, which acts as a stressed member of the frame.

The sports bike element of the MT-01 includes the front suspension, which is handled by fully-adjustable upside-down forks from Yamaha's R1 superbike. The brakes are R1-derived too, and the MT-01 also has another sports bike feature in the power-boosting EXUP valve.

At 240kg (529lb), the MT-01 is a monstrous and unique naked motorcycle.

The MT-01's huge engine and futuristic styling give it the look of a motorcycle that has just jumped out of the pages of a superhero comic book

→ supercharger. Despite that, the B-King could well be the most powerful naked bike ever produced.

KTM SUPERDUKE

Austrian company KTM made its name by winning numerous world titles for off-road racing, but the company's stated aim is to become the biggest bike manufacturer in Europe, and to this end it has started an assault on the market for street bikes.

Its first salvo in this campaign to conquer the streets was the Superduke of 2005, a sports-oriented naked bike with striking styling. Power comes from the company's LC8 engine, a 75° V-twin initially developed for the Adventure trail bike. For the Superduke, the capacity was enlarged from 942 to 999cc, giving 120bhp to propel the 179kg motorcycle.

An extremely compact and lightweight engine, the LC8 also benefits from a tailor-made electronic fuel injection system to maximise performance. It breathes through stylish twin underseat pipes which are slash-cut to match the bodywork.

The tubular space frame is specifically designed for the needs of a super-agile, high-performance street machine. Lightness and rigidity are the aims, and the bike's short wheelbase makes the Superduke a very quick-steering motorcycle.

All components that are not made in-house at KTM are top notch, such as the brakes and super-light 17-inch cast aluminum wheels which were developed specifically for the bike, both of which were produced by quality supplier Brembo.

The KTM Superduke is a classy, stylish naked bike with a price tag of £8345 in the UK (it will be available in the USA in February 2007).

KTM SUPERDUKE

SPECIFICATIONS

Introduced
2005
Engine
Water-cooled
75° V-twin
four-stroke
Capacity
999cc
Power
120bhp
Top speed
140mph

The KTM Superduke's looks are as sharp as its handling. The striking looks are backed up by top quality components and a thrilling ride

RETRO MOTORCYCLES

DUCATI PAUL SMART 1000

RETRO *Motorcycles*

If you love the looks of classic bikes but don't want to spend more time fixing and fettling a living antique than riding it, the bikes in the section are your perfect rides. They all have those classic looks but are modern motorcycles with all the engineering, safety and reliability benefits which that entails. Now who said you can't have your cake and eat it?

A quick glance at any of the bikes in this section could convince the casual observer that they are bikes from another era. With their old-fashioned style, redolent of machines from the 1960s and '70s, they resemble the classic bikes that old guys treasure and trundle out on the road on occasional summer Sundays.

But don't be fooled, these are thoroughly modern motorcycles underneath the looks. They are part of a trend that has been developing for a few years now in the world of motorcycling: the cult of the retro bike.

Motorcycle manufacturers have latched onto the fact that there are a whole lot of more mature riders out there who harbour a nostalgic yearning for the bikes they rode in their youth (or would like to have ridden). However, the reality of owning a true 40-year-old classic puts them off the idea: these bikes are crude, need lots of maintenance and feature antiquated engineering and dynamics.

The solution, exemplified by Triumph's 'Modern Classics' and Ducati's 'SportClassics' ranges, is to produce motorcycles that replicate the style of a bygone era, wrapping it around a motorcycle that has all the benefits of modern engineering.

The results are motorcycles which look cool ➔

KAWASAKI W650

SPECIFICATIONS

Introduced
1999
Engine
Parallel
twin-cylinder
four-stroke
Capacity
676cc
Power
50bhp
Top speed
93mph

→ but have reliable engines which do not leak oil, decent suspension and brakes and modern levels of comfort. In short, a classic bike that you can take out for a 100-mile run without needing a back-up guy with a full toolkit and a selection of spare parts!

KAWASAKI W650

The W650 was a modern interpretation of Kawasaki's W1 from 1966, a 650cc parallel twin which was Kawasaki's first four-stroke motorcycle, built in the style of the British bikes of the time such as Triumph's original Bonneville.

Kawasaki launched the W650 in the year 2000 to capitalize on the Japanese craze for classic bikes. Never intended to be sold outside its native shores, the bike developed such a cult following that demand forced Kawasaki to export the bike to Europe and the USA, which had their own emerging demands for such retro machines.

The W650's motor was the bike's centrepiece, a skilfully executed modern take on the parallel twins that were the signature of 1960s road burners. Its 676cc capacity produced a sedate 50bhp, tailored to give placid, usable power for mature riders.

Other period styling features were equally well rendered, with chrome fenders, rubber fork gaiters

The W650 was a modern interpretation of Kawasaki's W1 of 1966, which itself aped British bikes of the '60s like Triumph's Bonneville

and a tank badge which aped the 'mouth organ' emblem which was the trademark of classic Triumph bikes. The W650 was discontinued in 2005, and ironically it may well become as collectable as the original classics it seeked to imitate.

TRIUMPH SCRAMBLER

England's reborn Triumph company has turned the production of retro motorcycles into something of an art form over the last decade. Since the success of 1995's Thunderbird, a model built mainly to capitalize on the company's enduringly cool image in the USA, the company has defined the genre with a range of immaculate replica classics built with the benefit of modern engineering.

The latest of these is the Scrambler, which evokes all the Steve McQueen cool of '60s dirt bikes while providing a machine which can happily be used as an everyday commuter machine and doesn't feel out of place in the cut-and-thrust of modern traffic.

It is powered by the air-cooled 865cc parallel twin engine used in most of Triumph's other retro bikes, but detuned to produce a leisurely 51bhp. The emphasis is very much on providing usable pulling power rather than screaming top speed, allied to a slick five-speed gearbox which makes progress →

TRIUMPH SCRAMBLER

SPECIFICATIONS

Introduced
2006
Engine
Parallel twin-cylinder four-stroke
Capacity
865cc
Power
54bhp
Top speed
110mph

The Triumph Scrambler's high-level straight pipes and retro charm make it a winner with riders who hanker for a touch of Steve McQueen-style cool

TRIUMPH THRUXTON

SPECIFICATIONS

Introduced
2004
Engine
Parallel
twin-cylinder
four-stroke
Capacity
865cc
Power
69bhp
Top speed
115mph

→ along the highway a fuss-free affair. High handlebars and a wide, comfortable seat add to the relaxed air and make for a pleasant cruising vibe.

As an antidote to frantic sports bikes and today's frenzied pace of life, the Triumph Scrambler is an oasis of cool calm on which the rider can kick back and reflect on past times when life wasn't quite so hectic.

TRIUMPH THRUXTON

The Thruxton is a modern interpretation of the home-built English 'café racers' of the 1950s and '60s, bikes ridden by guys hopped up on the kind of adrenalin rush that only riding a machine capable of 100mph (the magic 'ton') could induce. These 'ton-up boys' raced from café to café, testing their bravado and high-speed skills as they went.

After Triumph's rebirth in 1991, and its subsequent re-establishment of itself as a modern motorcycle manufacturer, the company decided to draw on the heritage of its halcyon days of the 1950s and '60s, when parallel-twin engined roadburners like the Bonneville ruled the roads. The new Bonneville (see following pages) was born in →

With its classic style, the Triumph Thruxton is a beautiful evocation of the café racers popular with the 'ton–up boys' of the 1950s and '60s

SPECIFICATIONS

Introduced
2001
Engine
Parallel
twin-cylinder
four-stroke
Capacity
865cc
Power
62bhp
Top speed
100mph

Triumph
BONNEVILLE

Probably the most evocative name from Triumph's past, the Bonneville's comeback made it a hit two times over

The Bonneville T100's two-tone tank
marks it out from the standard model

*T*riumph took the time to re-establish itself as a serious manufacturer of modern motorcycles before re-activating one of its most famous model names of the past—the Bonneville. A decade had passed since the company's revival when the new born-again Bonnie appeared in 2001.

The original Bonneville's evocative name was derived from the famous Bonneville salt flats in America, scene of many record speed runs by cars and bikes. The new bike was designed to look like its namesake from 1968, which at the time was the fastest motorcycle in the world.

The new Bonneville may bear a striking resemblance to its illustrious forebear, but it is no road-burner like the old Bonnie. The 865cc engine which is common to the majority of Triumph's Modern Classics range delivers its 66bhp in a much more civilised way than the '60s Bonneville, with a subtle soundtrack emanating from its period-looking 'peashooter' exhaust pipes.

The T100 model pictured here takes the retro look one step further than the standard Bonneville,

with the most striking difference between the two being their gas tanks. While the standard model's tank is painted in a single colour, the T100 is graced with a two-tone paintjob with hand-painted coachlines in white or silver according to the base colour of the tank. In a neat personal touch, the underneath of each tank is signed by the craftsman responsible for painting it. The T100 outsells the standard Bonneville by four to one, reflecting the popularity of its full-on retro style

In keeping with its retro style, the Bonneville is one of the few bikes on the market today that are still fuelled by carburetors. A pair of electrically-heated Keihin carbs pass the fuel and air mixture into the engine, but Triumph has had to use a cunning ploy to keep the Bonneville within the European emissions laws which govern the amount of pollutants a motorcycle can kick out.

An air injection unit has been added near the spark plug to helps burn off unburnt fuel before it reaches the open air, but for 2008 Triumph will have to fit fuel injection to all its modern classics to make them emissions-legal.

→ 2001, and in the wake of the new model's runaway success it was only a question of time before the company got round to building a café racer version of the bike.

The Thruxton arrived in 2004, based on the Bonneville but with uprated and adjustable suspension to emphasise its more sports-oriented nature. This was also expressed in the Thruxton's engine: an enlarged version of the Bonneville's motor with bigger bores and pistons giving a displacement of 865cc and a power output of 69bhp (compared to the Bonneville's 66bhp).

The essence of the classic café racer look is reflected in the short-style front mudguard, rakish clip-on handlebars which combine with rear-set footpegs to set the rider in a racing crouch, and a distinctively racy speed hump on the seat.

The jewel of Triumph's Modern Classics range, the Thruxton oozes heritage and style. It's a bike the ton-up boys of the '60s would have been proud of.

RETRO FEVER

Seeing the success of Triumph's Modern Classics range, other manufacturers naturally wanted to get in on the retro motorcycles act, and in recent years there has been a steady flow of imitations, some with more of a classic influence than others.

The over-riding caveat with this type of machine, however, is that the bike's badge must have some heritage attached to it for the machine to have any credibility. Triumph pulled off its success with a masterly combination of retro styling and modern engineering, but crucially the marque had an established history which gave it iconic status, especially in the huge marketplace of the USA.

Other companies which did not have such an established status in the history of motorcycling found that their retro-styled products did not go down so well. There is one company which has fully embraced the concept of the retro bike, with the recent launching of its own series of classically-influenced machines benefiting from modern-day →

→ engineering. It is an Italian company with an evocative history in race and street bikes—Ducati.

DUCATI PAUL SMART 1000.

Ducati first showed its range of 'SportClassic' retro bikes at the Tokyo Show in 2003. The brainchild of Ducati design chief Pierre Terblanche, they are modern sports bikes with styling inspired by the company's fabled bikes from the 1970s. Two of the three-strong family of SportClassics hit Ducati dealerships in 2005, with the jewel of the range being the gorgeous Paul Smart 1000.

Produced in a strictly limited run of only 2000 for worldwide consumption, the bike announces this fact with tasteful 'limited edition' plaques. The bike is a tribute to the machine which Englishman Paul Smart took to a famous victory in the Imola 200 race of 1972.

As befits the top-of-the-range bike, it is fitted with top-quality, multi-adjustable Ohlins suspension front and rear. The Paul Smart 1000's fairing as well as the silver-blue bodywork and Sea Green paint on the frame echo that original race bike of 1972.

Attention to detail is staggering, epitomised by the tires which are shared by two of the bikes in the SportClassic range. To achieve a complete retro →

DUCATI PAUL SMART 1000

SPECIFICATIONS

Introduced
2005
Engine
Air-cooled
90° V-twin
four-stroke
Capacity
992cc
Power
92bhp
Top speed
120mph

The Paul Smart 1000 celebrates a famous Ducati race victory and exhibits the superb attention to detail that is the hallmark of the company's entire SportClassic range

DUCATI SPORT 1000

SPECIFICATIONS

Introduced
2005
Engine
Air-cooled
90° V-twin
four-stroke
Capacity
992cc
Power
92bhp
Top speed
120mph

→ look, Ducati approached Italian tire makers Pirelli who obliged by producing a modern version of its old Pirelli Phantom, complete with period tread pattern.

DUCATI SPORT 1000

Launched at the same time as the Paul Smart 1000, the Sport 1000 (inspired by the 1974 Super Sport 750 street bike) shares its basic chassis and engine, albeit in a slightly down-specced form.

The chassis is a traditional Ducati 'trellis' constructed from tubular steel, but with a design adjusted to suit the SportClassics' purpose. A conventional swingarm is fitted, but with only one shock absorber, to make room for the stacked twin silencers on the right of the bike. Forks are by Marzocchi with rear suspension by Sachs, replacing the quality Ohlins units of the Paul Smart. The swingarm itself is an asymmetrical design made from beefy steel tubing.

Power comes from Ducati's tried-and-tested air-cooled 992cc 1000DS 90° V-twin, as used in the company's Monster, Multistrada and SS models. Although not exactly a fire-breathing power plant, it provides enough go to make the bikes fun to ride.

As with all the SportClassics, gorgeous details abound: fork caps that have been buffed to give a

The Sport 1000 was inspired by Ducati's Super
Sport 750 of the 1970s and comes painted in
authentic period colours from that era

superb finish, an old-fashioned petrol cap and original 1970s typography on the white-faced instrument dials. It all adds up to a motorcycle that drips with heritage and design excellence.

DUCATI GT1000

The third model in the SportClassics range, the GT1000, arrived in dealerships in 2006. Ducati proclaimed it the most practical of the trio, as it was the only one to sport a dual seat to allow the rider to take a pillion passenger.

The bike uses the same engine as the other two SportClassics, and also shares the same basic chassis as the Sport 1000, apart from the fact that the GT1000 has twin rear shock absorbers to take the extra load of that pillion passenger.

Attention to period detail is similarly obsessive, with the alloy-rimmed wire wheels shared with the rest of the range. The Ducati name emblazoned on the tank is also an accurate representation of the original 1970s typeface.

A top-quality paintjob is another feature the GT1000 shares with its SportClassic stablemates. Not only does the lustrous finish look deep enough to dive into, it's also finished in genuine 1970s shades. Now that's attention to detail!

DUCATI GT1000

SPECIFICATIONS

Introduced
2005
Engine
Air-cooled
90° V-twin
four-stroke
Capacity
992cc
Power
92bhp
Top speed
120mph

The GT1000 is designed to be the most practical of the SportClassics, as it comes with a dual seat to allow for a passenger

CLASSIC MOTORCYCLES

TRIUMPH BONNEVILLE

CLASSIC *Motorcycles*

Not every old motorcycle can be considered a 'classic'. This status has to be earned, by the machine representing a great breakthrough in engineering, achieving racing success or by having excellent performance or styling – or all of these. Most of all, a classic has to exert an emotional attraction that can drive motorcyclists to preserve it for future generations to enjoy

How often have you heard the phrase 'they don't make 'em like they used to'? It's a common claim, especially from members of the older generations, and it can be considered the cornerstone of the classic bike movement.

The preservation and use of motorcycles from 'the good old days' is basically nostalgia on wheels. Some bikers get into it due to a yearning to recreate their lost youth, searching out the machines they owned (or wish they had owned) in younger years. Some delve even further back into the past to revive happy memories with machines owned by their fathers or older family relatives. Others just prefer the looks of older motorcycles produced in an age when things were simpler, before the likes of plastic and emissions controls were invented.

Whatever the reason, classic motorcycles are more desirable now than they have ever been. As collectible items, they tend to go up in value, especially as they are no longer being made.

The desire of many bikers to tap into the style of yesteryear is reflected in the popularity of retro motorcycles (see previous section). With these machines, buyers can associate themselves with those cool looks while enjoying the benefits of modern developments in motorcycle design. Of ➔

NORTON DOMINATOR 88

SPECIFICATIONS

Introduced
1952
Engine
Parallel
twin-cylinder
four-stroke
Capacity
497cc
Power
49bhp
Top speed
90mph

→ course, if you are a diehard classic fan, however, only the real thing is good enough...

NORTON DOMINATOR 88

Norton was renowned for its racing heritage, and was virtually invincible at the prestigious British Isle of Man TT races in the 1930s and '40s with its Manx Norton racer. The most famous of the Manx racers was created in 1950, when the works race bike was redesigned using an innovative tubular chassis.

During testing of the new machine, works rider Harold Daniell commented that it felt like riding a feather bed, and the name stuck—from that day on, the new frame, which gave excellent handling characteristics, was known as the Featherbed frame.

When the Featherbed frame was combined with Norton's parallel-twin motor in 1952, the company created the Dominator 88, hoping to produce the ideal combination of power and handling. This was the model which established Norton's reputation for producing twin-cylinder motorcycles with excellent handling.

The development of the Featherbed Dominators continued through the hotted-up 88SS and 597cc 99 models, culminating in the 650SS, with the parallel twin enlarged to 646cc. The latter was a serious

The Dominator 88 established Norton's reputation for making bikes with excellent handling

roadburner of the time, capable of achieving a top speed which was not far short of 120mph.

VINCENT BLACK SHADOW

With one of the most evocative names in the history of motorcycling and one of the most brutally beautiful engines ever, the Black Shadow towers above the classic world like a colossus. This legendary beast was indisputably the fastest standard motorcycle in the world when it emerged in 1948, and made a habit of smashing world speed records.

Based on the Vincent Rapide, the bike was powered by the company's formidable 998cc V-twin engine which, in Black Shadow specification, was capable of an astonishing 125mph top speed. The large speedometer, reading up to 150mph and specially produced by Smiths for the Black Shadow alone, served to emphasise this machine's performance prowess. The fact that the engine had an extremely sinister-looking black enamelled finish was also seemingly designed to warn the unwary of the ominous power that lay within.

Improvements implemented over the Rapide's engine to achieve an increase of 10bhp in maximum power and 15mph top speed included highly polished rockers, ports and combustion chambers and ➔

VINCENT BLACK SHADOW

SPECIFICATIONS

Introduced
1948
Engine
Air-cooled
50° V-twin
four-stroke
Capacity
998cc
Power
55bhp
Top speed
125mph

With a 125mph top speed, the Vincent Black Shadow was the ultimate roadburner of its day and unbeatable on the street

Brough
SUPERIOR

The rarity and sheer quality of this great leviathan
make it one of the most desirable vehicles on earth

The Brough Superior was renowned as the Rolls-Royce of pre-World War II motorcycles, and the legend of its most famous devotee–TE Lawrence, who achieved heroic status as Lawrence of Arabia–has ensured that the model's mystique is even stronger now than it was in its heyday. Lawrence's loyalty to the marque led to him owning no less than seven Superiors during his lifetime, while his passion for riding these fearsomely fast machines was ultimately to lead to his untimely death.

Brough's reputation for producing superbly built high-performance motorcycles was well

Lawrence of Arabia owned seven
Brough Superiors. This is the final
one, the machine on which he was
mortally injured in May 1935

BROUGH SUPERIOR SS100

SPECIFICATIONS

Produced
1924-1940
Engine
Air-cooled
V-twin
four-stroke
Capacity
996cc
Power
45bhp
Top speed
100mph

An earlier Superior SS100, note the tiny front brake for such a rapid bike!

earned. In fact, each machine was 'built' twice. After first being assembled to achieve a good mechanical fit, the components were disassembled before being painted or plated and going on to a final assembly process. Quality control was fastidious and heavily performance-based. The specification for the SS100 model favoured by Lawrence was for a top speed of at least 100mph, and if any finished example failed to reach that yardstick during testing it was worked on until it did, before being delivered to the customer.

The clientele that beat a path to company owner George Brough's door in Nottingham, England expected the very best from what was one of the most expensive motorcycles in the world at the time. They could also personalize their machine to their individual requirements, so each of the 384 Brough Superior SS100s made is unique. Lawrence's last motorcycle was fitted with all the best Brough equipment of the day, including Castle Brompton forks, Bentley & Draper rear suspension,

Royal Enfield brakes and Lucas electrics.

His mania for speed led him to push the bike's 1000cc V-twin engine hard. He also wrote of the strong emotional bond between man and motorcycle: 'Because Boa [Lawrence's pet name for his Brough] loves me, he gives me five more miles of speed than a stranger would get from him'.

Lawrence racked up over 25,000 miles on his final Superior (pictured left), and spent his last conscious moments on earth in the bike's saddle. Riding to his cottage at Clouds Hill one day in May 1935, he swerved to avoid cyclists and was pitched over the handlebars. With no helmet to protect his head, the injuries he suffered proved fatal after six days spent in a coma. The motorcycle escaped with relatively light damage and was repaired by George Brough himself. It still bears dents from the crash.

Rare and expensive in its day, the Brough Superior is now even more sought-after by collectors of pedigree machines, commanding up to seven-figure sums. Lawrence's is, of course, priceless.

→ high-compression pistons. A pair of big-bore Amal carburetors also exerted their effect on the bike's pace by increasing the amount of fuel mixture passing into those two gulping cylinders.

As well as being prodigiously powerful, the motor was also incredibly flexible, turning over at a leisurely 4,000rpm at 100mph in top gear, enabling relaxed high-speed cruising on roads where these kind of speeds could be achieved.

To enable the rider to rein in such high speeds, the Black Shadow inherited the Rapide's twin brakes for the front and rear wheels, with the drums uprated to a cast-iron ribbed pattern. The wheels were also easily detachable, an operation facilitated by the fact that the whole bike could be lifted clear of the ground when the main stand was used in conjunction with its twin side-stands.

That massive engine formed an integral part of the rolling chassis, suspended from a spine frame that doubled as a tank for the engine oil. Cantilever rear suspension featured a rear subframe which was pivoted from the rear of the gearbox against a pair of spring units arranged in a near-horizontal attitude. Rear friction dampers were located at the junction of the seat stays and the swingarm.

For the Series C version, introduced in 1949 (as pictured on page 141), the front end was fitted with Vincent's own 'Girdraulic' forks, which combined the rigidity of girder forks with the latest in hydraulic technology. In this system, a centrally-mounted hydraulic suspension damper acted in conjunction with springs contained in the pair of sleeves behind the fork blades.

As the power of the big V-twin Vincents made them ideal for hauling sidecars, the front suspension also featured an eccentric lower link which allowed the steering geometry to be adjusted to make it suitably tuned for this use.

But the legend and mystique of the Black Shadow is based on its effortless speed as a one-up machine, despite the dual seat. In the United States and Australia, it was the boss street racer, humbling →

→ anything from V8 muscle cars to the most highly-tuned Harley Knucklehead. That is why this extraordinary machine is such a revered and sought-after classic motorcycle.

BSA GOLD STAR DBD34

A truly legendary name in the world of motorcycling, the Gold Star took its name from a lapel badge awarded to riders who achieved a lap of 100mph at the famous Brooklands banked race circuit in England. In 1937, Walter Handley earned one of these awards for achieving a 107.5mph lap on a BSA Empire Star, and the next year's model was named the Gold Star in recognition of his achievement.

After the war, the model was relaunched, initially as a 350cc single-cylinder machine, in various forms from trials trim to track racer. The most famous Gold Star of them all, however, was the DBD34 which saw the light of day in 1956.

The DBD34 was powered by a 499cc single-cylinder engine with distinctive fins. The fact that the engine was an all-aluminum alloy unit set it apart from the more mundane BSA singles, which still used cylinder barrels made out of iron. The huge Amal 11/2-inch Grand Prix carburetor also stood out as a mark of the DBD34's sporting intent.

That sporting intent was realised in the year that the model was introduced, with the bike cleaning up at the Isle of Man Clubmans TT.

The top-of-the-range Clubman model came →

BSA GOLD STAR DBD34

SPECIFICATIONS

Introduced
1956
Engine
Air-cooled single-cylinder four-stroke
Capacity
499cc
Power
42bhp
Top speed
110mph

The Gold Star DBD34 was the ultimate café racer in the late '50s and early '60s

→ with race-style clip-on handlebars and a swept-back exhaust, and even the lower-specced models were soon being modified into the café racer style that was all the rage at the time. Clip-ons, bigger brakes and larger alloy tanks were the add-ons of choice amongst the British ton-up boys of the early '60s and the Gold Star, with its 110mph top speed, was the bike everyone wanted.

This was an uncompromising machine with a singular sense of purpose. Its tall gearing meant that slipping the clutch at speeds under 30mph was the order of the day. Combine that with an incredibly noisy exhaust note and you had a recipe for a thoroughly anti-social beast.

Once the rider got a lick on, the Gold Star really got into its stride, with 90mph possible in second gear, and the model really set a trend for fast riding. A 350 version was made available in 1960, but only to special order, and the when the 500 became too expensive to produce, the factory pulled the plug on the model in 1963.

But the Gold Star DBD34 is such an icon it refuses to die. Many have survived to become the cherished possessions of current owners, and the mere mention of the name is enough to give most classic bike fans a tingle down their spine. Parts are still being manufactured by specialist companies to keep BSA's sporting single going—and no doubt will continue doing so for many years to come.

The Gold Star is such a legend, no fan of classic British bikes ever wants to see it die.

NORTON COMMANDO 750

The big problem with the big parallel twin engines that were the flagship power units for British motorcycles in the 1950s and '60s was the inherent vibration which resulted from this configuration. A rider used to riding modern multi-cylindered machines would be shocked at the amount of vibes produced by, say, a '60s Triumph Bonneville.

The designers of the Norton Commando aimed to solve this problem with an innovative method →

Triumph
BONNEVILLE

A major success in its heyday, the Bonneville's name and profile make it an instantly recognizable British classic

The most famous of Triumph's motorcycles was named after the Bonneville salt flats in Utah, USA, where modified versions of the company's bikes had broken world speed records.

The original 'Bonnie' was basically a version of Triumph's Tiger 649cc parallel-twin-powered model with a modified cylinder head and twin carburetors to give extra performance. Aimed directly at the lucrative American market, its aim was to appease US bikers' demands for higher top speed, and after 1960, when a new frame which could better handle the extra power was introduced, the handsome Bonneville really took off as a popular roadburner with a 110mph top speed.

With a production run that lasted until the last days of Triumph's last-gasp workers' co-operative in 1983, the model proved to have incredible longevity. Despite regular updates, the basic design of the Bonneville remained the same, which was to prove its downfall in the end, along with the rest of the British motorcycle industry.

One of the most notable changes was the introduction of unit construction in 1963, with the engine and gearbox combined as one piece rather than being two separate units bolted together.

By 1972, Triumph estimated that it had built a quarter of a million Bonnevilles, and many were raced successfully, especially at the Isle of Man TT. Popular in its heyday, the Bonneville still exerts a unique attraction to fans of British bikes.

TRIUMPH BONNEVILLE T120

SPECIFICATIONS

Introduced
1959
Engine
Air-cooled
parallel-twin
four-stroke
Capacity
649cc
Power
46bhp
Top speed
110mph

This 1964 Bonnie features the uprated frame and forks introduced in the previous year

NORTON COMMANDO 750

Introduced
1967
Engine
Air-cooled
parallel-twin
four-stroke
Capacity
745cc
Power
58bhp
Top speed
115mph

→ of construction. The engine, gearbox, swingarm, exhaust system and rear wheel were mounted together on the bike as a single assembly, being attached to the massive tubular spine frame by three 'Isolastic' mounts. These rubber mounts served to soak up those irritating vibrations from the engine, creating a smoothed-out riding experience.

The concept worked beautifully, as long as the Isolastic mounts were kept in good condition, and soon after it was introduced in 1967 the Commando had gained a reputation as a quality machine. The steering and roadholding were well up to the standards set by the famous Featherbed-framed Nortons of the '50s, while the bike also had a decent

turn of speed. Its 748cc engine produced a decently healthy 58bhp to shift a respectably light 418lb (190kg) of motorcycle along the road and made for a 115mph top speed.

The bike's styling was also a big hit, with a sleek, lean look to it. The Commando Fastback which came in from 1969 was even cooler, with a radical style that made its contemporary the Triumph Bonneville look staid and old-fashioned.

Despite its popularity, however, by the mid-'70s the Norton Villiers Triumph (NVT) group which owned Norton was in serious financial difficulties. The Commando's swansong was the 850 Interstate MkIII model, which looked seriously outdated →

The Norton Commando solved the problem of vibration from its parallel–twin engine by soaking up the vibes with three rubber mounts

Commando steering and handling lived up to the reputation Norton had established with its Featherbed-framed bikes of the 1950s

→ when it emerged in 1975. It only lasted until 1978, when NVT went into liquidation, but the Commando still has a loyal fan base to this day.

HONDA CB750

Honda's CB750 heralded the arrival of modern motorcycling—and the future dominance of the Japanese factories—when it was released in 1969.

It was the first mass-produced four-cylinder bike the world had seen and came with an electric starter, disc front brake and a five-speed gearbox, an unparalleled specification for a production bike of the time—and all for a reasonable price.

This was the first real superbike, with its 736cc engine's four cylinders arranged across the frame, a format that has become a familiar trademark of most Japanese bikes ever since. Producing an impressive 67bhp, it gave the CB750 a 125mph top speed and proved the major attraction which made the bike a huge worldwide success.

Although it was a big and rather heavy bike, it offered levels of practicality and reliability that the owners of European and American motorcycles could only dream about.

The CB750 was not a revolutionary design; the only real innovation was the number of cylinders, →

HONDA CB750

SPECIFICATIONS

Introduced
1969
Engine
In-line
four-cylinder
four-stroke
Capacity
736cc
Power
67bhp
Top speed
125mph

In 1969 the CB750 was a fantastic package, with a reliable and powerful four-cylinder engine, electric starter, front disc brake and 125mph top speed

SUZUKI GT750

SPECIFICATIONS

Introduced
1971
Engine
In-line
three-cylinder
two-stroke
Capacity
738cc
Power
67bhp
Top speed
115mph

➔ but it was a great overall package and had a massive influence on the machines that followed.

SUZUKI GT750

Launched in 1971, the GT750 was Suzuki's first true superbike and made an immediate impact due to its rapid acceleration and radical design.

Suzuki had enjoyed success with racing two-strokes in the 1960s and decided to capitalize on that by creating a multi-cylinder two-stroke street bike. With the 738cc engine's cylinders arranged across the frame, water cooling was used in order to stop the middle cylinder from overheating. The bike was nicknamed 'The Kettle' in Britain and 'The Water Buffalo' in the United States due to this water cooling system, which was evidenced by the big radiator mounted in front of the frame downtubes and the smooth water jacket around the engine's cylinders rather than the usual fins.

The four-stage cooling system was relatively sophisticated for its day, with a thermostat blocking the flow of coolant when the engine was started so it could warm up quickly. As the temperature increased, other ducts opened to allow the coolant to flow and a electric fan cut in to aid cooling.

With a decent 67bhp, plenty of mid-range punch

Suzuki's GT750 was christened 'The Kettle' in the UK and 'The Water Buffalo' in the USA due to its use of water cooling for the engine

and a top speed of 115mph, the GT750 was a smooth, quiet, comfortable all-rounder rather than an out-and-out performance machine. Today, it is regarded as the most collectible production Suzuki.

KAWASAKI Z1

Honda's CB750 had changed the course of motorcycle development forever when it appeared in 1969, but the response from Kawasaki was a foretaste of the intense rivalry that would develop between the Japanese factories to produce the world's top superbike. Kawasaki had delayed and revised its own four-cylinder project when the CB750 was launched,

upping its capacity from a 750 to 903cc, and when the result, the Z1, was released in 1973 it trumped the Honda on capacity, technology and speed.

The Kawasaki's 82bhp engine made the Z1 a pure performance machine with a top speed of 130mph. It did this with the aid of double overhead camshafts, previously unheard of on a production bike and bettering Honda's single overhead cam design. The engine was bulletproof, too, with the Z1 establishing a new 24-hour speed and endurance record at Daytona, Florida in March 1973.

This, along with successes in other prestigious endurance races, prompted Kawasaki to offer a ➔

SPECIFICATIONS

Introduced
1973
Engine
In-line
four-cylinder
four-stroke
Capacity
903cc
Power
82bhp
Top speed
130mph

Kawasaki's Z1 out-performed Honda's CB750 thanks to its incredibly reliable double overhead cam four-cylinder engine. It really looked the part too

MOTO GUZZI LE MANS MKI

Introduced
1976
Engine
Air-cooled
90° V-twin
four-stroke
Capacity
844cc
Power
71bhp
Top speed
130mph

→ 12,000-mile, 12-month warranty on the model. Along with its breath-taking straight-line speed and the fact that the Z1 was far cheaper than rival European superbikes, this ensured the bike's popularity for most of the '70s. It earned the nickname 'The King' and established Kawasaki's enduring reputation for power and reliability.

MOTO GUZZI LE MANS

The new wave of Japanese superbikes may have had their European counterparts beaten on price, but when it came to style and individuality, the top Italian bikes were in a league of their own. One of the machines which epitomised this was the Moto Guzzi Le Mans of 1976. This lean, low sportster had the kind of aggressive beauty that made grown men go weak at the knees, backed up by a 130mph top speed and a deep, throbbing exhaust note from the huge 844cc V-twin engine.

That trademark Guzzi engine, with its cylinders arranged across the frame, meant that the Le Mans carried a lot of its weight quite high, giving it very responsive cornering characteristics. Moto Guzzi's new linked braking system was excellent, too, with the brake pedal activating the left-hand front brake disc as well as the rear disc, while the hand lever

Lean, low and aggressive, the MkI Moto Guzzi Le Mans is an Italian superbike classic that continues to stir hearts to this day

operated the right-hand front disc. Overall, the Le Mans was one of the finest superbikes of the '70s.

LAVERDA JOTA

The Italian firm of Laverda became famous for three-cylinder sports bikes in the early 1970s, with the powerful 3C model gaining favour after it was released in 1973. Three years later, at the request of the British Laverda importer, the factory produced a tuned version of the 3C, christened the Jota.

With performance camshafts, high-compression pistons and an exhaust that made virtually no attempt at silencing the thunderous noise of the 90bhp engine, the result was a big bruiser of a motorcycle with a 140mph top speed which could blow any other bike off the road. Numerous triumphs in production racing confirmed that the Jota was not a bike to be messed with and it soon gained a fearsome reputation as a mean roadburner.

Compared to other Italian bikes of the time, the Jota had very good build quality, with its main components over-engineered and subsequently heavier than most. The paintwork and chrome were of a good standard and many parts, particularly the instruments and electrics (widely regarded as the Achilles Heel of Italian motorcycles) were ➔

SPECIFICATIONS

LAVERDA JOTA

Introduced
1976
Engine
In-line three-cylinder four-stroke
Capacity
981cc
Power
90bhp
Top speed
140mph

The Jota was the ultimate superbike bruiser of the '70s. Its tuned three–cylinder engine made it the fastest production bike on the road in its day

sourced from Germany and Japan. The Laverda triple was modified in a number of different ways in the following years, including a smoother-running version with a different crankshaft and a 1200cc version. But none of them matched the brute power and raw sex appeal of the original Jota.

DUCATI 900SS

A pure-bred Ducati of the classic type, the original 900SS was essentially a production racer for the road. Built solely for speed, with every component geared towards that singular aim, there was nothing on the bike that didn't have to be there: no electric starter, no passenger seat, no creature comforts. Weighing in at a mere 188kg (414lb), it made its Italian rivals the Laverda Jota and Moto Guzzi Le Mans look like portly tourers.

Powered by an 864cc version of Ducati's V-twin engine, it featured the firm's race-developed 'desmodromic' cylinder heads in which the valves are closed by the camshaft rather than a spring. The engine was fed by huge, gaping 40mm Dell'Orto carburetors and breathed through extremely loud Conti exhaust pipes. The 79bhp motor was ➔

DUCATI 900SS

SPECIFICATIONS

Introduced
1975
Engine
Air-cooled
90° V-twin
four-stroke
Capacity
864cc
Power
79bhp
Top speed
132mph

Light, lean and powerful, the 900SS was the most focused of all the Italian superbikes of the '70s

Harley-Davidson
XR750

This bike has been a winner in American motorcycle racing for over three decades. And it keeps on doing the business

The XR750 is a racing classic and an icon of American motorcycle sport. Forget the rest of the world's obsession with superbikes and MotoGP racers, in America it's dirt track racing that pulls in the crowds—high-speed dicing and sliding on oval tracks with loose surfaces. And the XR750 is the undisputed ultimate master of the sport.

The model was introduced in 1970, when race team manager Dick O'Brien dropped a modified Sportster engine into the chassis of Harley's KR racer. Success only came when a new aluminum V-twin replaced the XR's iron-barreled engine in 1972, with Mark Brelsford taking the title that year aboard the revamped machine.

Since then, the XR750 has been virtually unchallenged as the dominant force in US dirt track racing, giving riders such as Jay Springsteen and Randy Goss the coveted number 1 plate. Scott Parker was the most successful of all, taking XR750s to an incredible total of nine National titles.

Since 1980, Harley-Davidson has not actually built complete XR750s, it merely sells the engines which are subsequently built up into complete race

bikes using components from companies such as frame specialists Champion.

The XR750 has a kind of brutal beauty that has become a timeless signature of the bike. Despite being well into its fourth decade, its look has hardly changed, despite a certain amount of development.

Today's bikes are fitted with upside-down forks, lightweight cast wheels have replaced the old spoked jobs and huge silencers are now the norm. Rear brakes have also appeared, where the old bikes had none at all, but the race bikes of today are still instantly recognizable as XRs.

Today's XR750s produce over 100bhp, with the racers reaching speeds of over 130mph on the mile ovals, making for a real macho-man sport and an awesome spectator spectacle, with the bikes bucking and weaving over the dirt.

The XR750 is as ingrained in US motor sport as the dirt that cakes the racers' faces. It is a true American classic.

This is the view most likely seen by racers not riding an XR750. The model has made winning American dirt track series a habit that other manufacturers have found it hard to break

HARLEY–DAVIDSON XR750

SPECIFICATIONS

Introduced
1970
Engine
Air-cooled
45° V-twin
four-stroke
Capacity
45 cu in (748cc)
Power
90bhp
Top speed
130mph-plus

→ slotted into a strong tubular steel frame which was firmly suspended by Marzocchi forks and shock absorbers, giving the rock-solid stability in corners that Ducatis are famous for. Brembo brakes and beautifully purposeful styling finished off the single-minded superbike package.

A very successful variant of the 900SS was the Mike Hailwood Replica, introduced in 1979. This was brought out to celebrate the legendary racer's win at the Isle of Man TT in 1978 after coming out of many years of retirement, an emotional achievement acknowledged as the greatest comeback in the history of motorcycle racing.

The bike's red and green livery over a fully-faired version of the 900SS with a race-style seat echoed Hailwood's Sports Motorcycles-built machine that took him to victory in that historic race. A 'Mille' version of the bike was later introduced with an enlarged 973cc version of the V-twin motor which featured a stronger bottom end.

The 900SS is in great demand today, reflecting the fact that it is the sleekest and most single-minded of the Italian superbikes of the 1970s. The Mike Hailwood Replica exerts a similar appeal, reflecting the glory of a great sporting achievement. They are both motorcycles of legend.

The Mike Hailwood Replica commemorated the great racer's triumphant return to the Isle of Man TT in 1978

CONTACTS

CONTACTS

APRILIA
www.aprilia.com

ARLEN NESS
www.arlenness.com

BENELLI
www.benelli.com

BIMOTA
www.bimota.it or
www.bimotausa.com

BMW
www.bmw-motorrad.com

BOSS HOSS
www.bosshoss.com

BUELL
www.buell.com

CAGIVA
www.cagiva.it

CONFEDERATE
www.confederate.com

DUCATI
www.ducati.com

FISCHER
www.fischer1.com

HARLEY-DAVIDSON
www.harley-davidson.com

HESKETH
www.broom.engineering.btinternet.co.uk

HONDA
powersports.honda.com

KAWASAKI
www.kawasaki.com

KTM
www.ktm.com

LAZARETH
www.lazareth.fr

MOTOCZYSZ
www.motoczysz.com

MOTO GUZZI
www.motoguzzi-us.com

MV AGUSTA
www.mvagusta.com

SUZUKI
www.suzuki.com

TRIUMPH
www.triumph.co.uk or
www.triumph.co.uk/usa

VICTORY
www.polarisindustries.com

VYRUS
www.vyrus.it

YAMAHA
www.yamaha-motor.co.uk or
www.yamaha-motor.com